Financial
Jiu-Jitsu

Financial Jiu-Jitsu

A FIGHTER'S GUIDE TO CONQUERING YOUR FINANCES

Scott Ford

WILEY

John Wiley & Sons, Inc.

Published by John Wiley & Sons, Inc., Hoboken, New Jersey.
Published simultaneously in Canada.

"Way2Wealth" is a registered trademark of Scott Ford.

For general information on our other products and services or for technical support, please
contact our Customer Care Department within the United States at (800) 762-2974, outside
the United States at (317) 572-3993 or fax (317) 572-4002.

Wiley also publishes its books in a variety of electronic formats. Some content that appears in
print may not be available in electronic books. For more information about Wiley products,
visit our web site at www.wiley.com.

Library of Congress Cataloging-in-Publication Data:
Ford, Scott.
  Financial jiu-jitsu : a fighter's guide to conquering your finances / Scott Ford.
    p. cm.
  Includes index.
  ISBN 978-0-470-64830-8 (cloth); ISBN 978-0-470-91069-6 (ebk);
  ISBN 978-0-470-91074-0 (ebk); ISBN 978-0-470-91075-7 (ebk)
  1. Finance, Personal. I. Title.
  HG179.F575 2011
  332.024—dc22

        2010018281

Printed in the United States of America
10 9 8 7 6 5 4 3 2 1

Contents

Foreword

Even when I started to feel ligaments tear and knew my arm was about to break, I stayed calm.

I was leading the match against Kazushi Sakuraba, but with about twenty seconds left I had made a mistake and gotten caught in a kimura arm lock. The kimura is a basic yet powerful submission hold; executed properly the elbow and shoulder are locked and when applied at full speed can easily dislocate the shoulder, rupture elbow ligaments . . . and break bones.

So I felt my arm start to go, but there was no way I was willing to "tap," which in fighting terms means to concede defeat.

Don't get me wrong. I'm not afraid to tap. Every fighter taps in training. We do it every day. That wasn't the problem.

You see, I had time to tap, but I just couldn't do it. Deep inside I had always wanted to answer the question, "Can I listen to a bone being broken and still not quit?"

I found out I could. Since I didn't tap, Sakuraba continued to apply more pressure, and suddenly my elbow audibly snapped. My arm was twisted at what other people have described as a horrific angle, but I kept my face as calm and composed as possible, mostly for the referee's benefit.

The referee looked at my arm, looked at me, looked at my arm . . . and I tried to convince him I was fine. I even said, "No, I'm okay . . . this happens all the time in training."

He didn't buy it. He stopped the contest.

Although I did lose the fight, I gained something incredibly more important than any victory I could have won. I learned, once and for all, that my mind truly is stronger than my body. Today, when things get tough, all I have to do is remember that if I can watch my arm get broken and still keep fighting . . . I can do anything. Our minds can be incredibly powerful tools if we let them.

That's why I agree completely with Scott's perspective, which you'll read about later, regarding the pain of discipline and the pain of regret. Scott's point is simple yet powerful: The pain of regretting what you didn't do or didn't try is so much worse than the pain of doing your best—in any situation.

I hope I never feel the pain of regret. In fact I love the "pain" of discipline because it ensures that I will never feel the pain of regret. (I say "pain" because doing the right thing for yourself and your family is never painful; doing the right thing is rewarding in and of itself.)

I know that if you try, anything is possible—for you, for me, for all of us. If you can dream it you can do it: In your personal life, your professional life, and in your financial life.

But you have to get started somewhere. I know. I'm not just a martial artist, an MMA fighter, and a passionate Brazilian Jiu-Jitsu practitioner. I'm a family man and a businessman as well. I spent the last years working to develop my schools so that I can provide for my family, teach Brazilian Jiu-Jitsu to future generations, and continue my family's legacy in the sport. Family is at the core of everything I do. I apply the same skills, the same discipline, the same drive and passion to building a financial future for my family that I bring to fighting.

Yet in all these areas the same principles apply. Think of it this way: Mixed Martial Arts is a blend of fighting styles and disciplines, but Brazilian Jiu-Jitsu is the backbone of MMA. Not a single great MMA fighter lacks Brazilian Jiu-Jitsu skills; even if you don't want to apply finishing holds you still must be able to defend against them. Ground skills are the backbone of any fighting art.

Along the way Brazilian Jiu-Jitsu showed me how to see life differently. It taught me to look at every angle, to be open to new ideas, to anticipate problems and seize opportunities. . . . Brazilian Jiu-Jitsu has taught me how to do things the right way by seeing the whole situation and choosing the right move.

Most important, Brazilian Jiu-Jitsu taught me to face challenges head on. If you face challenges, you learn . . . and those challenges are no longer new. There is no challenge you can't overcome.

Building wealth may seem impossible. It's not—at least it's not as long as you try.

You will achieve nothing if you don't try.

You can achieve anything if you try.

You may never step on a mat—and you may never have to wonder whether you should tap or not—but each of us fights to provide better lives for ourselves and our families. That's a fight we all want and deserve to win.

Scott will show you how.

RENZO GRACIE
Brazilian Jiu-Jitsu Black Belt
Owner and Chief Instructor,
Renzo Gracie Academies

Acknowledgments

Thanks to my wife Angie, for her constant love and support.

Special thanks to my pastor and church family, living reminders of the fact that any good resulting from this book—and from everything else in life—is a gift from God. He deserves all the thanks and praise.

In addition, I would like to extend my sincerest appreciation to the individuals directly represented in this book:

Alan Weiss, President, Regent Wealth Management Group

Jeff Rozovics, CPA, financial consultant and partner, Rozovics & Wojcicki; Brazilian Jiu-Jitsu Black Belt and gold medal winner of the 2004 Pan American Games

Jim Lake, National Sales Manager of Guardian Annuities, Brazilian Jiu-Jitsu Purple Belt

Luke Rinehart, Head Instructor, Clinch Academy

Mike Brown, former World Extreme Cagefighting (WEC) featherweight champion

Renzo Gracie, Brazilian Jiu-Jitsu Black Belt; Owner and Chief Instructor, Renzo Gracie Academies

Ron Carson, CEO and founder of Carson Wealth Management Group

Sam Sheridan, best-selling author of *A Fighter's Heart* and *The Fighter's Mind*

Thomas Ledwell, Special Operations Division Commander, Frederick Police Department; Brazilian Jiu-Jitsu Black Belt

Tom Hine, Managing Member of Capital Wealth Management LLC and 4th degree Shotokan Black Belt

Everyone at **Cornerstone Wealth Management Group** for their hard work, support, and dedication

Financial
Jiu-Jitsu

Introduction

I'm flat on my back and can't get up.

And I have him right where I want him.

In town for the week on business, my opponent stopped by the Clinch Academy in Frederick, Maryland, to work out and roll with some of the guys.

"Rolling" is the Brazilian Jiu-Jitsu version of karate's "sparring" without all the kicking, punching, and Bruce Lee vocal impressions. Brazilian Jiu-Jitsu is based on taking an opponent off his feet and using ground-fighting techniques and submission holds to defeat the other fighter. (That's why it's arguably the most effective martial art—most real fights end up on the ground at some point, and when they do, a Brazilian Jiu-Jitsu fighter enjoys a massive advantage.) Practicing the art "live" is commonly referred to as "rolling."

Now if you're picturing a Wild West gunfighter scenario where a gunslinger rides into town to challenge the sheriff, think again. Like almost everyone I've met associated with the sport, my opponent is a nice guy looking for a good workout, a little friendly competition, and the opportunity to test his skills—and himself—against others.

But he still wants to beat me. And I want beat him—even though as much as it pains me to admit he is bigger, stronger, and quicker.

In many athletic competitions those physical qualities create a significant and often insurmountable advantage. In most martial arts a larger opponent has the upper hand. (Greater reach and more powerful kicks and punches will do that for you.)

Brazilian Jiu-Jitsu minimizes the effect of some physical advantages. The ground is, in many ways, the great leveler. Reach is less of a factor when you and your opponent are both on the ground. Striking power is irrelevant in a sport where punches and kicks are not allowed.

What *is* allowed is the application of skill, strategy, technique, experience, flexibility . . . all the things you learn, over time, from skilled instructors—and from lots and lots of study and practice.

That's why I find myself on my back, in the guard position, holding my opponent between my legs and buying time while I get a feel for his skills and tendencies. Although other martial artists and wrestlers *hate* the idea of being on their backs—I know, because I wrestled for 10 years—within seconds I realize my best bet is to give away a small amount of control to my opponent in order to gain *greater* control of the fight. (Sound counterintuitive? By the end of the book it won't be.) So I use my legs to pin his hips and control his movements and my hands and arms to protect myself as I maneuver for position. In the guard I protect myself, exploring my options . . . and poised to seize opportunities.

Within 30 seconds or so I can tell he is relatively inexperienced but has also learned a few advanced moves he's dying to use on me. That's not uncommon in Brazilian Jiu-Jitsu; many people gravitate to the sport after watching Mixed Martial Arts (MMA) fights and are eager to try techniques used by the stars of the sport. (Imagine kids in a driveway channeling their inner Lebron James on a lowered basketball goal and you get the picture.)

And in many ways he's doing what so many people do in their financial lives. Think of it this way: Do you have friends who, for example, actively trade stock options in the hopes of striking it rich by using esoteric combinations of calls and puts . . . while they ignore the basics like living within their means and making smart investments so they can build lasting wealth and live the life they dream of?

I know people like that. And I bet you do, too.

My opponent—nice, smart guy that he is—has made that same type of mistake while we grapple. He has opted for flash over foundation; for sizzle over steak.

Keep in mind I'm by no means alone in recognizing the connection between Brazilian Jiu-Jitsu and personal finance. My friend Jeff Rozovics, a CPA and financial consultant, is a partner at Rozovics & Wojcicki, a highly respected accounting and financial services firm in Chicago, Illinois. Jeff is also a Brazilian Jiu-Jitsu Black Belt and gold medal winner of the 2004 Pan American Games.

In other words, he's no slouch in *either* field.

"In martial arts and personal finance, fundamentals are important," says Jeff. "Newcomers to Brazilian Jiu-Jitsu almost always want to learn advanced techniques without developing solid basic skills. They want to skip ahead and try something they saw on TV like a fancy throw or a cool submission move. Most people do the same where personal finance is concerned: They want to learn about things like trading commodities or foreign currency before they focus on having an emergency fund, keeping a budget, and building towards their retirement.

"Sadly, taking that approach usually means you'll fail. Fail in Brazilian Jiu-Jitsu and it's disappointing, but there are no lifelong consequences. Fail to build wealth and create a better future for your family and the consequences can be lifelong—and sometimes even tragic."

Here's the key: The core principles for success in Brazilian Jiu-Jitsu and in personal finance along with almost every other facet of life—are the same. You can apply those core principles even if you never step on a mat. After all, each of us "fights" the wealth battle— and each of us wants to *win*.

But do keep in mind that "winning" means different things to different people. My martial arts goal isn't to step into the Octagon with Renzo Gracie, one of the giants of Brazilian Jiu-Jitsu who continues to compete in MMA events, a remarkable individual you will meet later in the book. Instead I just want to continue to improve and test myself. Your financial goal is probably not to be the next Warren Buffett. Instead, your goal may be to put your children through college and build a nest egg so that you can retire early.

But no matter what, you need the right tools to help you achieve the goals *you* set and that *you* want to achieve.

And that's what I do. My opponent has already gotten frustrated with his lack of progress and starts to sit up to shift to a different position. For a brief second both of his hands are flat on the mat on either side of me.

I seize his wrist, unlock my legs, sit up quickly to the side, pass my other arm over his shoulder and arm, grab my wrist . . . and lay back, locking his body in place with my leg while lifting his wrist toward his ear. (If that sounds complicated it's not—the Kimura lock is a basic Brazilian Jiu-Jitsu technique taught at the beginner level.) Immediately he feels pressure on his elbow and shoulder. But not *too* much pressure.

My goal isn't to hurt him or anyone else I roll with. (If this had been a real fight I could have, though.) He's caught, he knows it—and he taps my arm with his free hand to signal his submission.

What happened? Size, speed, and age were nonfactors. I went in with a plan, protected myself, stuck to the basics, waited for an opening—and succeeded.

You can, too. Using the Way2Wealth, a financial planning process we developed at Cornerstone Wealth Management Group to help our clients pursue their financial dreams, I show you how to build a great financial foundation and then leverage that foundation to build wealth and work toward your financial goals. (We're pretty good at it; we have more than 300 clients and more than $150 million in brokerage and advisory assets under management.)

Best of all you learn how to deal with uncertainty and adversity, to overcome challenges, and to forge ahead no matter what happens in the market and the economy in general.

Fancy moves? *I didn't need them.*

Fancy financial techniques and strategies? *You don't need them.*

I promise. Turn the page and I'll prove it.

Scott Ford

CHAPTER 1

Prepare to Win—Now and Forever

*Problems are a part of life. I want puzzles to solve. I need problems
to solve. I want to take on problems I can't fix; if they have
solutions they are already solved. Problems make me think, push me,
and make me try harder. Recently I signed up UFC for six fights. I
did it to challenge myself. People flourish under pressure.*

Plus I love the sport too much to ever leave it.

—Renzo Gracie

I'm no Renzo Gracie.

But I don't feel bad. No one else is, either.

Who is Renzo Gracie? He's a member of the legendary Gracie family, the "first family" of mixed martial arts. While the Ultimate Fighting Championship (UFC) has certainly popularized mixed martial arts, the Gracie family embraced and then reinvented traditional martial arts and along the way revolutionized the art of fighting. It can be argued that without the Gracie family there would be no Mixed Martial Arts (MMA) and there would be no UFC.

Renzo is a Black Belt in Brazilian Jiu-Jitsu and helps run the world-renowned Gracie Academies, a series of schools around the world that teach Brazilian Jiu-Jitsu. He has competed for years, recently returning to the UFC, even though he's more than 40 years old, simply because, "I want problems to solve. Challenges make me better."

Renzo brings a variety of skills to every fight. In addition to Brazilian Jiu-Jitsu he has developed a broad range of strikes, kicks, and wrestling skills. Go to YouTube and check out highlights from his fights; he's a master at taking opponents to the ground, controlling them, and forcing submissions.

Renzo bases his entire fight plan on his ability to protect himself, when necessary, by falling back on his Brazilian Jiu-Jitsu skills—and using those skills to regain the offensive and regain control of a fight. His confidence and his ability to handle almost any situation are based on a fundamental set of fighting skills and principles.

In short, he's prepared—for anything.

And because he's prepared, he's able to react under pressure. In Brazilian Jiu-Jitsu and in personal finance, the most important skill you can develop is the ability to react under pressure. Watch an MMA fight or go to a gym and watch a Brazilian Jiu-Jitsu Black Belt in action. The best MMA fighters—and Black Belts—are always calm. They can find themselves in horrible positions, but they have trained themselves to remain calm, stay relaxed, and stick to their game plan. They don't panic because they're prepared, and that preparation gives them incredible confidence.

Preparation also helps them relax.

And stay objective.

Think about the financial meltdown our country recently faced; many investors panicked—and as a result froze. They had no "sell discipline" (you'll learn what sell discipline is later) and made horrible decisions based on fear instead of rational, objective decisions.

In Brazilian Jiu-Jitsu, our biggest enemies are our emotions and our state of mind.

In investing and personal finance, our biggest enemies are—that's right—our emotions and our state of mind. It's not the market, it's not the economy, it's us.

Your biggest enemy is *you*.

But it doesn't have to be.

The same approach Renzo Gracie and top Brazilian Jiu-Jitsu practitioners use—applied to personal finance and investing—will work for you, too. No matter what your current financial situation, no matter what obstacles you may encounter, no matter what changes in the market or financial crises you face . . . if you take care of the basics, stay calm, and don't panic . . . you *will* achieve financial success and you *will* reach your financial goals.

What is financial success? And how *do* you achieve it? You may think that achieving financial success (whatever "financial success" means to you, because it means different things to different people) is based on mastering complicated investment techniques.

It's not. Most people become wealthy because they do the little things right—time after time. They don't panic, and they don't give in to emotion. Instead they stay calm and focused, and they stick to their plans.

Financial Jiu-Jitsu is based on taking care of the basics first, using straightforward, easy-to-understand principles and strategies as a platform and springboard to future success. Of course, your financial plan will adapt and evolve as economic conditions change and you move through your life, but the guiding principles will never change. Renzo Gracie uses Brazilian Jiu-Jitsu as the foundation of his fight plan. Although he is certainly confident—justifiably so—in his punching and kicking abilities, his real confidence comes from knowing if those punches and kicks aren't effective he can fall back on his Jiu-Jitsu skills and regain control over the fight on the mat, no matter what his opponents throw at him.

Think of the following guiding principles as the foundation of *your* financial fight plan and the keys toward reaching *your* financial dreams—no matter what punches the market or the economy fires at *you*. If you follow these principles you should always react well in the face of adversity. Then, if you later decide to try more advanced investment strategies and techniques, go for it! You can add complexity, try new things, even take a few risks . . . secure in the knowledge that you constantly and consistently take care of the basics and are prepared to win any financial fight.

So what are your guiding financial principles? Here we go.

Give Back

I understand it might seem odd that the first principle of financial success is to give back. After all, isn't building wealth based on accumulating assets instead of giving assets away? (Of course, building "wealth" depends on your personal definition of "wealth," which you'll determine in Chapter 2, but for now you can assume "wealth" refers to financial and material assets.)

How do you succeed if you give away what you hope to accumulate?

I look at it differently. I think it's impossible to *get* what you are not willing to *give*.

Some people see giving back as a form of tithing. Spirituality is an important part of my life, and I tithe regularly. You may also. But even if you don't see giving back in religious or spiritual terms, you should plan to give back in a way that is personally meaningful to you.

For example, at the Clinch Academy where I train, we focus heavily on teaching and helping others gain Brazilian Jiu-Jitsu skills. We're all there to develop our skills by learning from instructors—*and from each other.* Stop by and you can see Brown Belts rolling with Purple Belts, Purple Belts rolling with Blue Belts, even Black Belts rolling with White Belts. Can a Black Belt, a person who has probably spent a minimum of 10 years perfecting his or her skills, learn from a White Belt who has spent less than a month practicing the sport?

Most of the time, the answer is yes.

Many people learn the most when they're teaching instead of being taught. Think of times you've trained another person to do a job or perform a task. I'll bet you ended up learning new things in the process.

In short, by giving back you also gain.

And you make the world a little better place. And feel good about it.

Plan to give back. Maybe what you can give is money. Maybe what you can give is knowledge. Maybe what you can give is time. Whatever you can give, I guarantee you will get back more in return—if not materially then certainly in terms of knowledge and self-satisfaction—than you ever gave.

Pay Yourself First

If you're living paycheck to paycheck, I'm sure you'll disagree with the next sentence.

Everyone makes enough money to be able to save.

That's right. *Everyone* makes enough money to be able to save—even if it's just a few dollars a week.

How can I say that with confidence? One, I've worked with hundreds of clients over the years, from young people just getting started to millionaires enjoying the fruits of their hard work and success. Their financial situations vary widely, but a common denominator is that all of them are able—even if it requires making a few changes to how they approach their financial life—to start saving money.

And here's the good news: Saving money doesn't require setting up and living by a budget.

Think of it this way. Say you move into a new apartment or a new house. It's bigger than your old place, and you don't have enough furniture to fill all the rooms. The first few weeks it feels a little strange as you walk around seeing all the empty space . . . yet before you know it each room is cluttered, your closets are full, and you wish you had a larger place.

What happened? *You filled the space.* The rooms were empty so you filled them.

In fact, you filled them almost without noticing.

The same thing happens in our financial lives. No matter how much money you make, over time you'll find a way to spend it. Think about the last time you got a big raise—for a couple weeks you felt "rich," but over time you grew accustomed to your new level of income, adjusted your lifestyle to fit your new level of income . . . and filled your financial house with furniture. The problem is that at some point you look around and realize the furniture you have isn't really the furniture you want.

In case you're wondering, the same thing happens in Brazilian Jiu-Jitsu. Every student learns new techniques and gains new skills. That's great, but most then spend more time learning more skills and learning more advanced techniques than on working hard to refine and perfect the skills they already have. At some point most take a step back and realize they collected a wide variety of techniques . . . but they aren't nearly as good at performing those techniques as they would like to be or need to be.

So how do you get out of this rut? How do you start saving when you currently live paycheck to paycheck? Do you—gasp!—create and live on a budget?

You certainly can, but you don't have to.

Instead of budgeting, get started by taking control. Start saving the simple way.

Pay yourself first.

Instead of paying your mortgage, paying your rent, paying your car payment . . . pay yourself. Pick a number. Maybe it's a set dollar amount. Maybe it's a percentage of your pay. I don't care what amount you choose, but always pay yourself before you pay anyone else. (In my opinion, you should always pay yourself 10 percent, but feel free to choose the amount that's right for you.) Fill your savings "house" with furniture first and *then* worry about filling all the other rooms with financial "furniture." You'll quickly adapt to your new "living conditions" and will adjust your spending accordingly—and your net worth will grow.

Worried you won't have the self-discipline to pay yourself first? No problem. It's easy to pay yourself first when you . . .

Automate!

The easiest things to do are the ones you don't have to think about doing. The easiest choices to make are—you guessed it—the ones you don't have to think about making. Paying yourself first is easy if you only make that choice once.

Automate the process of saving—that's easy. Make the choice every week or month? That's much harder. I know—it's hard for me, and it's hard for my clients. A small percentage of my clients have the discipline to write a check every month and deposit funds into their investment accounts; everyone else—including some of my wealthier clients—has set up an automated process that automatically transfers funds. Paying yourself first is hard to do consistently.

That's why the key is to set up a system that makes paying yourself first automatic.

The most common example of an automated process is to have money deducted from your paycheck for deposit into your 401(k) plan. If you've done so (and if not, why not?), think back to when you first set that process up. Say you decided to put 3 percent of your pay aside for retirement. The first time you saw your paycheck, you were probably a little disappointed that your take-home pay was slightly lower than it had been before the deduction. But after a couple paychecks you stopped thinking about the reduction and adapted accordingly. No pain—and over time a lot of financial gain.

All because you paid yourself first—and made the process automatic.

I discuss a variety of savings and investment strategies later; for now, just embrace the concept of paying yourself first and setting up automated systems to make it easy. Electronic banking and Web-based financial services make it simpler than ever.

The easy way is always better . . . when the easy way is also the most effective way.

Maintain a Cash Safety Net

Most financial experts feel you should maintain an emergency fund to cover true emergencies: Losing a job, unexpected medical expenses . . . things outside your control you must—absolutely *must*—have cash in order to cover. (A 70-percent-off sale does not constitute an emergency.)

I agree. Not just because an emergency fund makes good financial sense, but also because a cash safety net can give you peace of mind. Think back to Renzo Gracie; he doesn't worry about whether his striking skills can carry him through a fight. He prepares for other outcomes by knowing he can rely on his Brazilian Jiu-Jitsu skills.

Instead of *worrying* about things that might go wrong, *prepare* for the possibility things might go wrong.

And sleep better at night.

So what is your goal for your financial safety net? The most common advice is to have three months' worth of expenses in a savings account. Think about what you spend on a monthly basis, multiply by three—and there you go.

I think three months' worth of expenses is a great goal, but it's also somewhat simplistic and a little unrealistic for most people, especially people just getting started taking control of their financial lives. If you spend $3,000 a month and currently have no money in savings, the thought of setting aside $9,000 probably sounds impossible.

A better approach is to decide what you *have* to spend. If you lose your job, for example, some of your expenses will be lower, like gas and food. If you lose your job, you might decide that some of today's "necessities" are no longer quite so necessary.

So take a step back, think about your situation, and come up with a number that's right for you. Maybe it's $5,000. Maybe it's $500. Whatever it is, start putting aside money—automatically—and fund your cash safety net.

Then don't use your cash safety net unless you absolutely have to; and if you ever do, replenish it as soon as possible.

Manage Credit Wisely

Ah, credit. We all have it. We all use it.

We all secretly hate it.

Credit is not a necessary evil. Credit is actually an incredibly useful financial tool if managed wisely.

But most people don't manage credit wisely. The average U.S. household with at least one credit card maintains a balance of more than $10,000.

Ouch.

The problem is that most of those people will be paying that debt off for years—even decades. Credit card issuers *want* you to maintain a balance; they make most of their money on interest payments. The longer you maintain a balance, the more interest you pay, and the more money the card issuer makes . . . and the more money comes out of your pocket. Say you're better off than the average U.S. household and you only owe $8,000 in credit card debt; if your interest rate is 18 percent and you make the minimum payment every month you'll end up paying almost $20,000. In effect, whatever you originally purchase eventually costs you two-and-a-half times what you paid!

That's managing credit unwisely . . . and paying for a mistake for a *long* time.

And that's like trying an advanced Brazilian Jiu-Jitsu technique when you haven't even established a good base; in a real fight you would pay for a mistake like *that* for a *long* time.

On the other hand, most of you borrow money when you buy a house. If you buy a house you can afford, get a loan at competitive terms, make your payments on time, and—depending on interest rates—even work to pay off your loan early, that's managing credit wisely.

The key is to ensure that the credit you use fits within your overall financial plan and helps you build wealth. Credit should not be something you fall back on because you *want* to; credit should be a financial tool employed as the result of an informed and intelligent financial decision.

Few people manage credit wisely.

You will.

Get Time on *Your* Side

Time is arguably the most powerful component of any investing plan—and often the most overlooked.

Think I'm wrong? Here's a quick example.

Say you have $10,000 to invest. Assume you earn 5 percent per year on that $10,000 investment. Five percent is a conservative amount; I chose a conservative amount to prove my point. You won't add additional funds; over the life of the investment your only contribution will be the initial $10,000.

Then let's say you invest that 5 percent in a tax-deferred IRA; any earnings will not be taxed until you withdraw them. Now factor in time; here's what your original $10,000 will be worth. After:

10 years	You'll have: $16,289
20 years	You'll have: $26,533
30 years	You'll have: $43,219
40 years	You'll have: $70,400

(Keep in mind this illustration is not representative of any specific investment.)

Notice the effect of time and compounding. As time passes, your account grows, and the interest you earn increases because it is factored against a larger base dollar amount. For example, after 20 years you earn interest on more than $26,000 instead of on your original $10,000. The relatively low interest rate didn't change; your investment value did.

That's the power of time—and compounding. Even at low rates, you can build incredible wealth.

The same principle applies in most areas of life. It starts in school; you learn basic math and then leverage your knowledge to learn algebra, geometry, calculus, and so on. It takes time, and over time your knowledge grows and compounds. As you grow in your career, you gain experience and skills you leverage; but gaining that experience takes time.

In fact, earning higher-level Brazilian Jiu-Jitsu belts is in large part based on time—not necessarily elapsed time, but based on hours spent actively mastering the sport. Students learn new techniques over time. They apply those techniques to skills and strategies they have already mastered . . . and compound their knowledge and abilities.

All by taking advantage of the incredible power of time.

If you feel like time is against you, think again. It's never too late to start. Take control and make time work *for* you. Every wealth-building- and investment strategy that makes up the Way2Wealth is based on harnessing the power of time and compounding. Think of time as an opportunity, not as a regret, and you'll succeed. Any goal you wish to reach can be accomplished much more easily when you get time on *your* side.

Never Procrastinate

Waiting is the worst approach you can take in terms of building wealth.

Let me repeat that. Waiting is the worst approach you can take—especially when you know what to do . . . but just don't do it.

Procrastinating is the polar opposite of getting time on your side.

Why? Time is only on your side when you take action and let time work its magic; for example, like when you invest in a 401(k). Once you make the investment, time starts working for you. Until you do . . . time is against you. Say you wait 10 years to invest $10,000 in a retirement account, as in the example above. After 40 years you've lost almost $30,000 in earnings—simply because you procrastinated.

Here's the bottom line: If something is worth doing it's worth doing *today*. Not tomorrow. Not next week. Not next year.

Today.

Don't agree? Think about procrastination in personal terms. Think about some of the things in your life you regret most. Do you regret the things you've done? If you're like most people, you regret a few of the things you've done, but that's not where most of your regrets lie; I firmly believe that if my heart is in the right place things will work out for the best, even if in the short term I think I have made a mistake.

Instead, most people regret the things they *didn't* do—or waited too long to do. I wrestled from the age of 5 up to high school and was successful. I really enjoyed the sport and have never regretted being a wrestler. But as I look back I wish I had gotten started in Brazilian Jiu-Jitsu earlier; it quickly became a passion and a sport I will practice for the rest of my life. (After all, think how good I would be now if I had started a few years sooner!)

Many of you look back and wish you had done certain things . . . sooner.

Most of you look back and wish you had done certain things . . . *period.*

Don't let that be you, especially where your financial life is concerned. You don't have to be wealthy to enjoy the fruits of a positive, balanced financial lifestyle. Building wealth and taking control of your financial life will help you, your family, your community . . . even if you don't become rich, you will certainly be able to live a richer, fuller life.

Stop procrastinating *today*. And in the future, never procrastinate when you know the right thing to do. Take steps. Make changes. Do what needs to be done to reach your goals and live your dreams. Although taking certain steps may be slightly "painful" in the short term—for instance, if you put money aside to build your Cash Safety Net instead of buying clothes—you'll be that much farther along to living the life you really want to live.

Think of it this way. There are two types of pain: The pain of discipline and the pain of regret. Discipline weighs ounces; regret weighs a *ton*. Take the time now to identify your goals; at the end of that process you may decide you need to set aside $200 per month in order to meet those goals. That's a little painful . . . but if you don't, and 20 years from now realize that to meet your goals you need to set aside $5,000 a month, that's incredibly painful. Setting aside $200 a month weighs ounces; setting aside $5,000 a month weighs a ton.

Which is worse? The pain of discipline or the pain of regret?

I'll take discipline any day.

Never look back and say, "I wish." Look forward and say, "*I will. Starting today!*"

Make Reality Your Perception

I know. You think I have that backward. Most people say, "Perception is reality." In many cases that phrasing is true; for example, if people perceive you as a good person their assumption and perception is their reality.

In financial terms, perception often is not reality. Think about all the sources of financial information available to you. On a daily basis you can quickly get overwhelmed by all the "experts" spouting their advice on TV, in newspapers, magazines, on the Web. . . .

Most are loud. Most are certain. Most claim to have all the answers.

Most are wrong.

If they weren't wrong, they would all be rich—and the rest of us would be, too.

A number of people train regularly at the Clinch Academy. New people come in all the time. I roll with many of them, and in the process we share ideas, concepts, techniques, and strategies. Sometimes I learn new things; much of the time I listen while applying a huge grain of salt.

Why? I'm always open to new ideas and definitely feel I can learn from everyone, but I mainly rely on the instruction and advice I receive from Luke Rinehart, the head instructor and owner of the studio. He has the credentials, he has the expertise, he has the knowledge—and just as important he has the ability to make the complicated simple and the difficult easy.

I can turn to Luke for the right answers.

In short, I have learned I can trust him.

Sifting perception from reality in the financial world can be much harder, especially if you listen to too many voices. The key is to find sources of information and advice you can trust. To build wealth, you won't have to pour over reams of financial data every day. Later I'll show you how to build a team of financial professionals you can trust.

The key is to know reality when you see it and to make decisions based on accurate information and accurate advice. That's what smart investors do—and over time smart investors tend to become wealthy investors.

Follow a Simple and Comprehensive Strategy

Ever read a contract? I'm sure you have.

I'm also sure you noticed all the complicated and esoteric legal jargon that probably only makes sense to lawyers. In actuality all those complicated phrases and clauses have a real purpose, but it's easy to assume words like "herewith" and "heretofore" are used just to make what should be easy seem really hard.

Sadly, many people in my profession do the same thing. They make building wealth and achieving financial freedom seem incredibly difficult, when in fact it really isn't. Don't get me wrong: Effectively managing money for a high net-worth investor can include diversifying assets, taking advantage of tax shelters, creating a blend of equity and speculative instruments, investing in commodities and precious metals . . . all the pieces and parts can be complicated.

But it's not hard—as long as you know what you're doing.

The same applies to anyone, regardless of his or her current net worth. The key is to follow a simple strategy that takes into account all aspects of your personal and financial life. No matter how much money you have, the basic principles are the same:

Use strategies that seek to minimize risk, maximize return, and build a smart plan that helps you pursue your individual goals.

That's it. Simple. Comprehensive. Easy to follow.

My goal is to help you unclutter your financial life, build a solid base, react and respond based on knowledge and plans, and enjoy life knowing you will reach your goals—and will never need to panic.

Let's build a plan for you!

Prepare to Win—Now and Forever

If you do nothing else, follow these guiding principles to help build a better financial life. Follow these principles in other aspects of your life and you'll succeed in those areas, too. Work hard enough and someday you might challenge Renzo Gracie; if that happens let me know because I'd love to be there. If you ever find yourself unsure of what direction to take, check out this list. I feel sure the answer is here.

- Give back.
  Help others, and you will always receive more than you give.
- Pay yourself first.
  Build for tomorrow by taking action today.

- Automate!
  Don't think, don't decide—automate!
- Maintain a cash safety net.
  Even if a rainy day never comes, you'll be ready.
- Manage credit wisely.
  Make credit a useful tool instead of a necessary (and expensive)
      evil.
- Get time on your side.
  Time is the greatest tool at your disposal; it works for you even
      when you're sleeping.
- Never procrastinate.
  The pain of discipline weighs ounces; the pain of regret weighs
      a ton.
- Make reality your perception.
  You don't have to know everything; you just need to know—and
      trust—the right people.
- Follow a simple and comprehensive strategy.
  Building wealth isn't hard, but it will mean sticking to a
      smart plan.

Ready? Let's start building your individual strategy!

2

Balance and Base

WHAT IS TRUE WEALTH TO YOU?

I wrestled in high school and college, and while I can land shots, I definitely focus on getting opponents on the mat where my grappling skills give me an advantage. That's where I'm often at my best. When I first got started in the sport I thought I knew everything I needed to know, but when I decided I wanted to become a champion I realized I had to put in a ton of Brazilian Jiu-Jitsu work. For me it all started with knowing where I wanted to go; when I made it my goal to be the best, everything I needed to do followed. That day, I realized "good" wasn't "good enough."

—Mike Brown

In Brazilian Jiu-Jitsu, everything starts with balance and a good base. Everything. Every technique, every strategy, every hold . . . everything is based on establishing a good base and staying in balance. If you're off balance you're out of control . . . and you have almost no chance of success. A good base is everything.

—Luke Rinehart

I love goals.

Goals are like a road map . . . but much better. Sure, they help you know where to go, but they can do much more. Goals can get you up in the morning, keep you going when times are tough . . . goals are a reason to not just exist but to truly *live*.

If you're like me you have many goals. Mine are fairly basic. I want to live my faith. I want to be a great husband and father. I want to help my company—and more important our employees—grow and prosper. I want to help our clients reach their goals. I want to get a little better, each and every day, at Brazilian Jiu-Jitsu. In the largest sense, I want to make the world a little better place and in the process glorify God.

And at this moment, I want to help you reach your goals.

But before you get started, keep this in mind:

True Wealth is made up of all the things money can't buy and death cannot take away.

So let's figure out what True Wealth means to you; in the process you'll determine your goals, and you'll start to build a blueprint for your own simple, comprehensive financial strategy. Later you'll figure out how you'll get where you want to go—first you'll determine where you want your journey to take you.

Step 1: Forget Financial Goals (At Least for Now)

That's right: Forget financial goals.

Why?

Financial goals should be a by-product of personal goals, not a goal in and of themselves.

Think about it. Which goal gets you charged up more?

- I want to have a million dollars.
- I want to see my children live happy, healthy, and fulfilled lives.

If you're like me, helping your children trumps becoming a millionaire any day.

For example, say one of your goals is to pay for your child's college education. What an admirable goal; not only will your child benefit, but imagine how wonderful you will feel watching your son or daughter get his or her diploma on graduation day.

Providing a better life for your child is a tangible goal you can see and touch and embrace because it strikes an emotional chord within you.

Simply wanting to be a millionaire doesn't have nearly the same emotional impact.

So, your first step is to identify what is truly important to you and set goals based on those key drivers. *Then* you'll work on creating financial goals and a financial plan that helps you support the goals you set.

Try this. What:

- Do you value most: spiritually, emotionally, in terms of family?
- Motivates you?
- Principles and ethics do you use to guide the decisions you make?
- Do you want to achieve for yourself and your family?
- Is your mission in life?
- Would you like to be remembered for?

Most of you don't look at your lives that way. The pace of everyday life makes you incredibly short term in nature; you make decisions and plans based on what you need to accomplish today, tomorrow, and sometimes, if you're lucky, next week.

It might sound like a morbid thought, but think about your eulogy. (If you like, write what you hope will be said at your funeral—that might be the best "mission statement" you'll ever create.) What would you like the person delivering your eulogy to say? Would they discuss money? Would they share stories and anecdotes about your houses, boats, cars, or bank accounts?

No. (I sure hope not.)

Pretend a family member is delivering your eulogy. How can you ensure they will be able to say the things you really want them to say? It's actually easy. All you have to do is:

Live with purpose by thinking and acting with the end in mind.

Take a moment and think about your legacy. What would you like to leave behind? Not in terms of assets or wealth, but in terms of the impact you make on the people you care about. What do you hope you can do for your family? What do you hope you can do for your church or community? How would you like people to remember you and the life you lived?

Building your legacy is accomplished by achieving goals that serve your long-term desires and vision. Focus on the wrong goals and you won't build the legacy you want. Sure, you will have achieved things . . . but will you have achieved the things you *really* want to achieve?

The only way to know is to answer the question: What is true wealth to you?

So let's answer it.

Step 2: Develop Your Vision for Your Life

Let's take a quick step back. Imagine you're Mike Brown and you just got started in mixed martial arts. Your first day in the gym is overwhelming; you're a great wrestler, but you have an incredible amount to learn about other fighting techniques: punches, kicks, throws, submission holds, Brazilian Jiu-Jitsu . . . for just about anyone that first step in the gym could be incredibly intimidating. (I know it was for me.)

Then imagine you're Mike Brown and you've decided you want to become a Mixed Martial Arts (MMA) champion. Talk about an overwhelming prospect for someone with limited mixed martial arts experience!

But then again . . . maybe not so overwhelming. Becoming a champion requires a tremendous amount of skill, effort, experience, and plain old hard work . . . but a number of those skills can be quantified. Mike could have broken down his major goal into intermediate goals and short-term goals, and after some effort developed a comprehensive plan, that admittedly would need to evolve over time, all leading him to his ultimate goal.

I'm guessing that's exactly what he did. No one becomes a champion through luck.

You can reach your dreams, too. Start with where you want to go, determine where you are today, and fill in the gap.

That's what goal setting and planning is all about.

You'll start with where you want to go—not in terms of money or wealth, but with your dreams for yourself and your family.

Take plenty of time and fill in the following sections. Don't be tempted to skip this important step; determining your vision for your life sets the stage for everything that follows. One day you will look back and be glad you took the time to do a little soul-searching and dreaming; the discomfort of discipline always beats the pain of regret.

My Personal Goals

_____

_____

_____

_____

_____

_____

_____

_____

_____

_____

_____

My Goals for My Family

_____

_____

_____

_____

_____

_____

_____

_____

_____

_____

_____

My Ideal Career or Vocation

_____

_____

_____

_____

_____

_____

_____

_____

_____

I Would Like to Spend My Free Time . . .

_____

_____

_____

_____

_____

_____

_____

_____

_____

_____

_____

If I Only Had 3 Months to Live, I Would . . .

_____

_____

_____

_____

_____

_____

_____

_____

_____

_____

_____

_____

If Money Were No Object, I Would . . .

_____

_____

_____

_____

_____

_____

_____

_____

_____

_____

_____

I Would Like to Give Back By . . .

_____

_____

_____

_____

_____

_____

_____

_____

_____

_____

_____

_____

I Most Want to Be Remembered for . . .

_____

_____

_____

_____

_____

_____

_____

_____

_____

_____

_____

_____

Did you run out of space in any of the categories? If so, great! If not, grab a few pieces of paper and revisit each category. Building a vision for your life can be fun—dream big!

Step 3: Determine Your Specific Goals

Now go back through your list and create concrete goals for each category. In some cases creating concrete goals might be a little tough; for example, you may have listed "Was kind and generous to everyone he met" in the category "I Most Want to Be Remembered For." Being consistently kind and generous is a wonderful quality to aspire to but is a little tough to create goals around; in effect it is instead a principle and set of ethics you wish to live by.

On the other hand, if you listed "Pay for my child's college education" in the "My Goals for My Family" section, that's a concrete goal that you can both measure and quantify; you'll either have the money or you won't (and they'll either go to college or they won't). Good goals are achievable and measurable; focus on identifying goals you can get your arms around.

Then apply a number to those goals. Not a number in terms of priority but in terms of what each goal will cost to achieve. In some cases it will be easy; for example, currently the average tuition cost at a public college or university is a little more than $7,000. That's an easy goal to quantify and get your arms around. (You can prioritize later if you like.)

Other goals might be tougher to quantify, but not if you put some thought into the process. Say you want to "retire" from your current job at age 50 and start a second career as a teacher; you can quantify that goal by doing a little math. If you currently make $60,000 and teaching pays $50,000 you'll need to make up the $10,000 difference either by cutting your current spending or by putting aside some savings to draw from (or possibly both). Grab a calculator, jot down a few numbers, and see what you come up with. Not only will you put a number to a goal, but you'll also think critically about what you hope to achieve and what steps you're willing to take to reach your goals.

Below is a worksheet you can use to help guide you. On the left fill in quantifiable goals; on the right, estimate the cost of achieving the goal. Don't worry if the dollar figures are large numbers with lots of commas and zeros; you'll figure out how to overcome hurdles later.

For now identify what you want for yourself and your family. Pick goals you can touch, feel, and taste.

Why? You'll do anything to achieve the goals that touch your heart.

Goal	Financial Requirement
_____	_____
_____	_____
_____	_____
_____	_____
_____	_____
_____	_____
_____	_____
_____	_____
_____	_____

If you need more space feel free to continue on another sheet of paper. Just keep in mind the purpose of this exercise is to identify large, overall goals; if you wrote, "Get one month ahead on my house payment" with a financial requirement like "$900" you've probably gone into too much detail. If that is the case, change the goal to something like, "Pay off my house five years early" with a financial requirement of "$4,000 or $100 per month."

When you're done, you should have a comprehensive breakdown, at least at a high level, of your long-term goals and the financial requirements or impact of those goals.

Now take a step back. Do your goals tie in with the vision you created for your life? Did you stray into areas that don't tie in?

For example, did you throw in purchasing a new boat in as one of your goals? If you did, that's certainly okay . . . as long as your overall vision included something like, "Purchase a house on the lake for family vacations and for our kids to use when they get older." If having a lake house to provide a way to bring your family together is important to you, great! That's a goal you can touch, feel, and taste. If having a lake house is only important because you'll get an ego boost from telling friends about your lake house . . . it's a goal you'll never get behind and will probably never achieve—and if you do achieve it, most likely you'll do so at the expense of another goal that someday would have been more important to you.

Again, think of your eulogy. Which would you prefer your son to say?

"Dad lived a great life; he worked really hard and bought a house at the lake," or

"Dad lived a great life; he worked really hard to find ways to bring the family closer. I remember all the times we got together as a family at the lake house . . . we'll cherish those good times, and every time we go there we'll remember what an impact he made on all of our lives."

The first statement is all about ego; the second is a heartwarming, touching remembrance delivered by a person you truly care for.

And that, my friends, is an example of True Wealth.

If this process didn't leave you charged up and excited about building a better future for yourself and your family, then the vision you created and the goals you set haven't touched you emotionally. Work back through the vision categories and goal-setting exercise again. Always start with the end in mind—and make sure that end is one you truly embrace and would do anything to achieve.

If the "why" is big enough . . . the "how" is easy.

What Is True Wealth to You?

Determine what True Wealth means to you. Think in terms of things money can't buy and death cannot take away from you. What legacy do you want to leave?

- Set the stage—set financial goals aside (for now).
  Money can't buy love or happiness or anything except . . . *things*.
- Determine your vision for yourself and your family.
  What will your eulogy be? Start shaping it now.
- Determine your specific goals.
  Turn your vision into concrete goals you can touch, feel, and taste.

Don't move on to the next section until you feel great about your vision and your goals—always start with the end in mind!

CHAPTER

Closing the Gap

ANALYZE YOUR CURRENT SITUATION

I train our officers in self-defense and incident control. Many of our officers have a martial arts or wrestling background, but dealing with dangerous, real-life situations can be incredibly stressful. We employ a variety of Brazilian Jiu-Jitsu techniques to help control situations while keeping our officers safe—and causing minimal injury to others. We start with determining what basic skills each person brings to their training—and then we fill in all the gaps. While they may be hesitant at first, especially when they realize how much they need to learn, by the end of their training our officers are much more confident and assured . . . and it shows in their performance.

—Thomas Ledwell

Closing the gap is one of the trickiest moments in Brazilian Jiu-Jitsu; the possibilities for what can happen are almost endless. So is the potential for the unexpected. I used to worry a lot about what my opponent might do; later I realized if I focus on what I want to do and what I want to control, what my opponent might do is almost irrelevant. Go into every fight with your own plan and execute your plan—that's the best way to close the gap and ultimately to win.

—Luke Rinehart

approach Brazilian Jiu-Jitsu the way Luke does (which makes sense because he's my instructor; I'd be a terrible student if I didn't follow his guidance).

For example, say I know I'm really strong from the top position. Or say I have a great butterfly guard. On the other hand, say I also know my weakness is getting caught in triangle chokes.

If the above is true (and it's not, because if you come to my gym the last thing I wish to do is provide you with a scouting report), it only makes sense for me to do everything possible to take advantage of my strengths while avoiding my weaknesses.

Knowing my strengths and weaknesses helps me build a game plan that I will follow regardless of who my opponent may be.

The key to closing the gap is to objectively analyze the situation and develop a reasonable game plan. In Brazilian Jiu-Jitsu we train to overcome weaknesses while making sure our strengths remain our strengths—and as a result we close our personal gaps while we close the space.

Space in Brazilian Jiu-Jitsu is a problem: Space creates greater opportunity for escapes, submissions, and uncertainty. In Mixed Martial Arts (MMA) terms, closing the gap can be a real problem if you're not good on your feet; although you try to take your opponent to the ground, you're open to devastating kicks, punches, and other strikes.

Space is a problem—in Brazilian Jiu-Jitsu and in personal finance. So let's close the gap.

Before You Close the Gap: Overcome Your Fear of the Unknown

Familiarity doesn't breed contempt; in my opinion it breeds comfort and certainty. The more I know and master in Brazilian Jiu-Jitsu, the less nervous I am about rolling with someone new . . . and the less hesitant I am to try new things.

Here's a quick example: The kick-over sweep, a fairly flashy technique performed from the bottom, closed guard position, looks impressive and works well, but requires perfect timing, finesse, and using an opponent's movement and strength against him. Performed properly it's a beautiful move; performed incorrectly—or at the wrong time—it's a recipe for disaster.

For a long time I avoided trying a kick-over sweep "live." Sure, I practiced it . . . but against willing, cooperative "opponents."

Then I realized the only way to overcome my hesitancy was to dive in, take a few risks, and learn from my mistakes. After all, what did I *really* have to fear?

What's a little embarrassment among friends?

So I practiced and worked and experimented. I looked stupid a time or two (or more, to be honest). I failed. I tried. I failed again. But I kept trying and in the process overcame my fear of the unknown as I broke the technique down into small, bite-size steps I could master. In the process I learned a little more about myself and my abilities, improved on a weakness, and closed the gap between the unknown and the known.

The first time I pulled off a kick-over sweep live I was thrilled. It wasn't perfect but it *worked*. What had seemed impossible now seemed almost effortless.

I closed the gap and turned my fear of the *unknown* into a sense of comfort with the *known*.

I feel sure you have at least one financial fear causing you stress and anxiety. Maybe one fear is what will happen to your credit card interest rate if you make a late payment. Maybe you worry about what you'll do if you lose your job—or what will happen if your overtime gets cut and your monthly income goes down. Or maybe you are concerned about long-term issues like whether you'll have enough money to retire comfortably.

Those are all reasonable and understandable concerns. But they don't have to create fear or even stress.

You already took the first step toward closing the gap—you identified your vision for your life and your concrete goals. The second step in closing the gap is to analyze your current situation so that you'll know where you're starting from; then you'll work to close that gap so that you can reach your dreams.

Step 1: Forget about Budgets

That's right. You heard me. Forget about budgets. I hinted at this earlier, and now I'm saying it.

Why? To be honest I'm not a big budgeting guy. Sure, my wife and I know our monthly expenses. We know what we spend, know what we save, know what we put aside for a rainy day . . . but we don't live by a budget. We spend money on the things we feel are important, and we save money in order to build our vision for our family and to ensure that we leave the legacy we want to leave.

But we don't live by a budget.

You don't have to either. In fact, some of my wealthiest clients have never budgeted. They make smart financial decisions, sure—but they don't budget.

Never have, never will.

But if you'd like to create a budget, please feel free. Some people swear by them, and if you feel that creating and following a budget will help you, by all means do so. Everyone has individual strengths and weaknesses, and everyone uses different tools to help them succeed.

My point is, however, that if you don't want to create a budget, don't. Put your effort in other activities instead.

Step 2: Make Sure You Have Positive Cash Flow

Again, you don't need to live by a budget—but you do need to bring in more money than you spend. Otherwise how can you build wealth?

The key is to have a positive cash flow, which is just another way of saying you earn more than you spend. If you're making cash advances on credit cards in order to pay your normal monthly expenses, then you don't have positive cash flow. Sure, there's money in your pocket (at least for the moment), but you're going further into debt to finance your current lifestyle.

So let's figure out your cash flow. Again, this isn't a budget; it's an easy way to determine whether you spend more than you earn—

and if you do, to determine where you can cut a few expenses so that your cash flow is positive.

Income

How much do you make? You may not know exactly how much you spend, but I bet you know how much you make. For now, ignore your gross income and focus on your take-home pay. (Your gross income is *nice* to know, but you can't spend your gross income; all you can spend is your net income.) If you're married, by all means include your spouse's income; also include any child support you receive, pension income, and so forth; if it is money that flows into your household on a regular and reliable basis, include it.

Write your net income here: $ _____

Expenses

Now the process gets a little more involved—but not much. Most people don't have a good handle on their expenses. In a moment, you will. Fill in your amounts on the following worksheet.

Expenses Worksheet

Mortgage/Rent	_____
Car payments	_____
Credit card payments	_____
Car insurance	_____
Gas and car repairs	_____
Home insurance	_____
Other loans	_____
Life insurance	_____
Child care and tuition	_____
Groceries	_____
Utility bills	_____
Phone bills	_____
Internet	_____

(Continued)

Expenses Worksheet (Continued)

Cable bill   _____

Clothing   _____

Meals (out)   _____

Entertainment   _____

Other   _____

Total Expenses $_____

See? That wasn't so hard. Then the rest is easy:

Income $ _____ minus Expenses $ _____ = $ _____

If the result is a positive number, even if just by a dollar, you have positive cash flow.

If the result is a negative number your cash flow is negative. You're spending more than you earn; you aren't closing the gap, but instead are creating a bigger gap each and every month.

In Brazilian Jiu-Jitsu terms . . . as well as in financial terms . . . *ouch.*

If your cash flow is negative, you have two choices: Increase your income or decrease your expenses. (Actually you have three choices; you could increase your income *and* decrease your expenses.) The problem for most people is that increasing income, at least in the short term, is hard. Decreasing expenses, on the other hand, can be as easy as changing a few habits.

So: If you have negative cash flow, before you move on determine how you will change your financial lifestyle and habits so your cash flow will be consistently positive; otherwise, not only will you never have more than you have now . . . over time you'll actually have *less.*

Step 3: Create a Personal Balance Sheet

Once you establish the state of your monthly cash flow, it's time to determine your net worth. Pretend you're a small business—or even a corporation—and create your own balance sheet. A balance sheet is simply a financial report listing the assets and liabilities of a company, or an individual or family. The difference in what you *own* and what you *owe* is your net worth, or your personal balance.

See? Balance is important in all aspects of life—not just Brazilian Jiu-Jitsu.

Here's the formula:

$$\text{Assets} - \text{Liabilities} = \text{Net worth}$$

Let's start with your assets. Assets are cash or items that can be turned into cash.

For example, bank accounts, stock investments, retirement accounts—all are assets.

Your home is also an asset as long as it has equity, which means it is worth more—in terms of real market value—than what you owe. If you could sell your house for $300,000 and you only owe $250,000, your equity is $50,000. That equity is an asset. The total value is not an asset; just the amount of equity you have in the home.

If your car is paid off and you could sell it for $8,000, it's an asset. If you just bought a car and you put little or no money down, even though it's "worth" $25,000, it's not an asset because if you sold it today the proceeds will not go into your pocket—the money will go toward paying off your loan.

If this sounds confusing, don't worry—the process of creating a personal balance sheet will sort out any confusion.

Use the following worksheet to list all your assets. Fill in the amount for each category. Remember, an item's value is what you can sell that item for, not what it is theoretically "worth." A silver necklace that cost $400 isn't worth $400 unless you could fairly easily find someone ready, willing, and able to pay $400.

Personal Assets Worksheet

Cash   _____
Checking account   _____
Savings account   _____
Money market funds   _____
Home(s)   _____

(Continued)

Personal Assets Worksheet (Continued)

Life insurance (cash value)	_____
Stocks	_____
Mutual funds	_____
IRA	_____
401(k)	_____
Automobiles	_____
Jewelry	_____
Antiques and collectibles	_____
Other	_____
Total Assets	$ _____

List everything, but again, don't be tempted to overestimate values. It's easy to place emotional value on an item that has no bearing on its actual value. For example, your grandfather's old pocket watch may be priceless—to you—but in reality may only be worth $20 to someone who did not have a relationship with your grandfather.

Think of it this way: If you died and all your possessions had to be sold, what would they be worth?

Once you've listed your assets, it's time to list your liabilities.

Liabilities are what you owe. Any debt is a liability: credit cards, personal loans, mortgages, car loans . . . even money you owe to friends or family.

Determining your liabilities is easier than determining your assets. In most cases you get a bill or a statement unless a friend loaned you some money. (Regardless, a personal debt is still a liability.)

Use the worksheet below to list your liabilities.

Again, list everything. Take the time to think it through. It may be a painful and depressing exercise, but don't be tempted to hide from reality.

Remember, in order to effectively close the gap you have to start from where you are today. To reach your goals you first have to understand your current situation—that way you can take steps to improve your situation and start building toward achieving your personal vision and goals.

Personal Liabilities Worksheet

Mortgage	_____
Credit cards	_____
Automobile loans	_____
Medical bills	_____
Personal loans	_____
Student loans	_____
Store loans (furniture, etc.)	_____
Alimony and child support	_____
Other	_____
Total Liabilities	$ _____

Now that you know what you own and what you owe, simply subtract your liabilities from your assets to determine your net worth.

Total Assets $ _____ minus Total Liabilities $ _____ = Net Worth $ _____

For example, if you have $100,000 in assets and $80,000 in liabilities, your net worth is $20,000.

The greater your net worth, the better off you are . . . but even if you have a negative net worth (meaning you owe more than you own), don't worry—the Way2Wealth will put you on the right path.

A simple premise to keep in mind: It's easy to assume that you have a high net worth if you have equity in your home. Say your home has a fair market value of $300,000 and you only owe $250,000. The result is an asset worth $50,000. Wait—not so fast. You have to live *somewhere* . . . so can you really access that money in an emergency? Maybe so, maybe not . . . just don't be tempted to think you're in great shape because you have money in your home. Even if you sell the home to tap the equity, you'll still need a place to live, and you'll have to spend some amount of money for housing.

Determining your net worth may not be a fun exercise, but it's an incredibly valuable exercise that helps change your mind-set and sets the stage for you to follow the Way2Wealth.

Step 4: Keep in Mind the Total Financial Picture

Cash flow and net worth provide a great look at your current financial situation, but they don't complete the total financial picture. Other items fill in the remaining gaps. For example, you may not currently have sufficient insurance coverage, or you may have too much. Or you may have a pension plan that will provide income when you retire; that pension plan may not be an "asset" today, but it certainly will be in the future.

For now you won't have to dig deeply into those subjects; you'll fill in the gaps in your comprehensive financial plan as you move through subsequent chapters. (For example, in Chapter 8 you'll make sure that you have the right types and amounts of insurance coverage for your individual situation.) For now know that you've gone a long way toward closing the gap. Later you'll take care of a few additional details.

So what have you accomplished? You've analyzed your current situation and closed a huge gap. You know where you stand and where you want to go. How do you get there? By setting a Family Benchmark—that's next!

Closing the Gap

Know your strengths, know your weaknesses, and overcome your fear of the unknown—all without becoming a slave to a budget! Everyone starts somewhere, so if you don't feel great about your starting point, don't worry—the Way2Wealth will provide you with the tools and strategies to dramatically improve your financial situation as you work toward realizing your dreams.

- Forget about budgets.
  Be smart and have a plan, but spend effort where it makes sense for you.
- Make sure you have positive cash flow.
  Spend less than you make, and you can build wealth.

- Create a personal balance sheet.
  Know what you own and what you owe—that's one gap you'll
    work to increase.
- Fill in the gaps later.
  Keep in mind that you'll build a comprehensive financial plan as
    you follow the Way2Wealth.

What's next? You learn to forget about external benchmarks like
the Dow Jones Industrial Average, the prime rate, or the federal funds
rate. Instead, I'll show you how to create your Family Benchmark.

CHAPTER 4

Family

YOUR FAMILY BENCHMARK

*I think the most important thing in life is gratitude. Be happy
with what you have. Don't focus on what you don't have, but
inventory what you do have. Then face forward, not backward. If
you wake up every day feeling fortunate to have what you have,
then you can move forward and achieve even more. Here's what I
always try to do: If I have a tough day, I try to remind myself what
I have that other people around the world don't have and possibly
never will have.*

—Tom Hine

*A couple of years ago I re-evaluated my approach. I was teaching
martial arts skills but I wasn't happy with the environment in the
studio. I realized that if I wanted to create an atmosphere of mutual
respect between all of our students, that attitude had to start with
me. So I looked at my goals and realized I had to change what
I did—even if just in subtle ways—to make sure I helped build the
kind of environment I want. Every student has different goals, and
that's great. While I teach martial arts, my real objective is to help
each person reach their goals while also making sure they walk out
the door feeling better about themselves than when they walked in.*

—Luke Rinehart

Reaching goals, in Brazilian Jiu-Jitsu and in any other aspect in life, involves following a clear path. In Chapter 2 you decided where you want to take your life; in Chapter 3 you took an objective look at where your journey will start.

I feel sure that the process was at least partially eye-opening and a little humbling, just like the first time any of us roll for real in the gym. We all tend to think we're in better shape—financially and physically—than we really are. But that's okay; as Renzo Gracie told me,

> We are naturally afraid of what we don't know and can't control. Every time a small child goes into a new environment, he holds his parent's hand, then walks a few steps, tests the environment, walks a little farther . . . every time you walk into a different environment you are naturally insecure about how you will be perceived, how you should behave . . . but grappling teaches you to acknowledge you're in a new situation and to be confident. When you face life, you learn—and over time new situations are no longer scary . . . they are just new. And exciting.

So if analyzing your current situation was a little depressing, again—that's okay. Now you know where your journey begins. You know the environment. You don't have to be afraid of the unknown; you know exactly where you stand.

Better yet you know your destination. You know what you want to achieve for yourself, for your family, and for your community. You set concrete, specific, attainable goals.

Now let's take steps to try to reach those goals.

Your Family Benchmark: An Introduction

Flip back to Chapter 3 for a moment, and take a look at your goals. Each goal included an estimate of the money needed to accomplish that goal. For example, if one of your goals is to pay for your child's education, you estimated how much money that would take. If you decided that someday you want to live on a beach, you estimated a dollar amount required to enable that lifestyle. If you want to change careers someday and work for a cause you're passionate about—but that calling doesn't pay as well as your current job—you came up with a number.

It's all about numbers.

But not in the way you might think.

Take a look at almost any personal finance book, and you'll notice the authors take a similar approach. Say one of your goals is to save for your child's education. You estimate you'll need $80,000. Your child is 4 years old, so you have 14 years to save that much. Eighty thousand divided by 14 is a little more than $5,700; that's how much you need to save each year to reach your goal if you don't earn any interest or any return on your savings.

Here is the calculation:

> To reach $80,000 in 14 years at a 0% rate of return
> you need to save $5,700 per year.

(Keep in mind that this equation and the equations to follow are not representative of any specific investment. These assume you will earn a stable, fixed rate of return, but it is important to recognize that some investments are subject to fluctuation and there is no assurance a stable rate of return can and will be maintained.)

You can earn some return on your savings, though, even if you simply stick them in a bank savings account. In fact, let's see how putting your money in a savings account could turn out. As I write this, many banks offer rates of approximately 1.25 percent on passbook savings.

Let's do the math:

> To reach $80,000 in 14 years at a 1.25% rate of return
> you need to save $5,200 per year.

So what happened? Just by earning 1.25 percent on the money you put away, you reduced the amount you need to save by $500 per year. That's $7,000 less than you originally estimated.

Let's go a little farther. Say you average a 6 percent rate of return:

> To reach $80,000 in14 years at a 6% rate of return
> you need to save $3,600 per year.

A 6 percent rate of return dropped the amount you need to save per year by $2,100, or more than $29,000.

I could keep going, but I'm sure you get the point. Once you set a financial goal—once you pick a number you want to reach—what really matters is your rate of return. If you make $30,000 a year it might be really tough to put $5,700 each year into a college fund. But if you can get a 6 percent return on your savings, you will only need to save $3,600 each year.

Although that still might sound like a lot, it's much less daunting than $5,700.

And if you can average an even higher rate of return, the amount you need to save to reach your goal continues to decrease. For example, if you can achieve an 8 percent annual rate of return you will only need to save $3,060 per year.

Think of it this way. You need to earn money to save money. (Obvious, I know, but work with me for a moment.) Most of you do not have a tremendous amount of control over the amount you earn. If you are paid by the hour, and you don't have the opportunity to work much overtime, your annual pay is predictable. If you are a salaried employee, you know how much you will make this year.

In either case you can ask for a raise, but there is no guarantee you will receive one . . . and if you do, the amount is likely to be small. Again, most people don't have much control over their rates of pay. So achieving a higher rate of return on savings is in a way like giving yourself a raise because you reduce the amount of money you have to earn—and save—to achieve a particular goal. Although you may not be able to ask your boss for a $2,500 raise, if you achieve a higher rate of return, you don't need to save as much.

All of which leads me to two simple principles. To reach a specific financial goal:

The more you can save, the lower the required rate of return.
The less you can save, the higher the required rate of return.

Your ultimate goal is to save a lot *and* achieve a high rate of return. But the problem is that you can't always control how much you save. Situations change, circumstances change, the unexpected occurs . . . life happens.

That's why your Family Benchmark is *not* an amount of savings per month. Your Family Benchmark is *not* what might seem like an impossibly high savings target. (If you decided you need $1.5 million to reach your goals, I understand if today that sounds impossibly high.) Your Family Benchmark is the rate of return you need to achieve to reach your goals. You may not always be able to control how much you bring home. You might not be able to control how much you save. But if you stay focused and get the right people in your corner, you can over time enjoy a fair amount of control over your rate of return. You may do better in some years than others, but over time smart investors who take advantage of expert guidance from skilled, experienced advisors tend to have a much better chance of reaching their goals.

Your Family Benchmark is your "required" rate of return. Not a dollar amount, not an end goal, but what you need to earn on your investments to reach your goals. Focusing on your Family Benchmark makes it easier to adapt to a changing environment, because your Family Benchmark can naturally be more flexible than a fixed rate of pay or a fixed amount of annual savings.

The Family Benchmark in Action

I will work through an example in a moment so you can see why I feel that the Family Benchmark is such a useful financial planning tool. But first it might be helpful to think about the Family Benchmark in Brazilian Jiu-Jitsu terms.

Say a new member—call him John—joins the Clinch Academy. He's been in the sport for a few years, has heard about Luke, heard about the Academy, and feels it's the right place for him to continue to develop his skills. On his first day a number of us are rolling, and Luke pairs me with John so he can assess John's skills.

I don't know John's skills in Brazilian Jiu-Jitsu. In fact, I know nothing about him other than that he seems like a nice guy. I don't know how strong he is, how flexible he is, or how experienced he is. So I'm cautious at first, I stick to the fundamentals, and I focus on achieving balance and maintaining a good position.

Within moments I realize two things: He's stronger and more flexible than I am. (Sadly, time takes its toll on all of us.)

Now think about my situation. He's stronger than I am, and there is no way I can instantly become stronger. He's more flexible than I am, and even though I can certainly handle the pain of muscles and joints stretched beyond their normal limits, in the long term risking a muscle tear is a foolish approach.

So what *can* I do?

I can take advantage of my experience (now the effect of time *is* on my side) to use what I *can* control to adapt to conditions I *cannot* control. I can shift subtly and use leverage to overcome his greater strength. I can control my position so he can't bring his greater flexibility into play. Most importantly, I can relax, stay patient, and use my experience to seize the right opening.

I can adapt to a new environment.

The same happens in the investment world. You may not be able to increase your salary. You can call that your "strength" because it forms the basis of your everyday finances. You may not be able to increase the amount you save—call that your "flexibility" because how much you save will naturally vary depending on your salary and your expenses. But you *can* benefit from knowledge, experience, and expert guidance to use the skills you learn to seize the right openings and to take advantage of changing economic and financial market conditions.

The rate of return you achieve is based largely on skills and experience, not on strength. Not on what you earn. Not on how much you save. We're all different—different incomes, different expenses, and different goals. What I have is not what you have; what I dream of is not what you dream of. But we can all apply skills and experience to work hard to achieve a rate of return that helps us reach our goals—no matter where we start from or where we want to go.

Time and the Power of Compounding

The Family Benchmark is based on a simple premise: Time and the power of compounding are your best investment friends. (Well, that and an outstanding rate of return. I get to that in a moment.)

When you invest, time adds value to your money. Here's a quick example: watch what happens to $10,000 as the years pass. You can assume that you earn 5 percent per year, a relatively low (historically) rate of return, and that you don't add any money to the account other than the original $10,000.

If You Invest $10,000	You Will Have	Increase per 5-Year Period
In 5 years	$12,700	$2,700
In 10 years	16,300	3,600
In 15 years	20,800	4,500
In 20 years	26,500	5,700
In 25 years	33,900	7,400
In 30 years	43,200	9,300

Notice two items in the chart. One, your savings grew from $10,000 to $43,219, an increase of more than $33,000, simply based on the power of time and compounding. Compounding occurs when the amount you earn—in this case 5 percent—is added to your original investment. Over time you earn that same 5 percent on a larger amount of money, which means your total dollar returns are higher.

That's the second item to notice—scan down the Increase per 5-Year Period column and you can see that the dollar return gets higher each time. In the first period your savings increased by $2,700; in the last period they increased by more than $9,300 because the 5 percent rate of return was applied to a much larger balance.

Over time, your earnings are reinvested, earn more, are automatically reinvested again, earn more, are reinvested . . . the cycle continues and the impact becomes ever more dramatic as the years go by.

Your money grows and grows . . . without your having to do a thing. (Other than leave it alone and enjoy it from afar, of course.)

Want to see a more dramatic example of the power of time and compounding? Let's set a higher Family Benchmark; let's assume you will invest the same $10,000 but this time will enjoy an 8 percent rate of return:

If You Invest $10,000	You Will Have	Increase per 5-Year Period
In 5 years	$ 14,700	$ 4,700
In 10 years	21,600	6,900
In 15 years	31,700	10,100
In 20 years	46,600	14,900
In 25 years	68,400	21,800
In 30 years	100,600	32,200

The results are dramatically different, even though in the first five-year periods, possibly not so much. For example, in the first five years your account grew by $2,700 at 5 percent and by $4,700 at 5 percent. Two thousand dollars is certainly nothing to sneeze at, but take a look at the last 5-year period. Instead of growing by $9,300 at the 5 percent rate, your account grew by $32,200!

That's the result of compounding: Your earnings were automatically reinvested, and your rate of return applied to that higher amount.

Your initial $10,000 grew to be worth more than $100,000—due solely to the power of time and compounding. What would you rather have, $43,200 or $100,600?

It's an easy choice to make, isn't it?

Just for fun, add another piece to the puzzle. Say you have $10,000 to invest, can add $2,000 per year to the account, and enjoy an 8 percent annual rate of return. Then the power of time and compounding will produce an incredibly dramatic effect:

If You Invest $10,000 (and $2,000 annually)	You Will Have	Increase per 5-Year Period
In 5 years	$ 27,400	$ 17,400
In 10 years	52,900	25,500
In 15 years	90,400	37,500
In 20 years	145,500	55,100
In 25 years	226,400	80,900
In 30 years	345,300	313,300

After 30 years, instead of $100,600 you end up with more than $345,000 in your account, a difference of $245,000! Keep in mind a basic difference in this example compared to the other examples. Over the course of 30 years you also added $2,000 per year, or $60,000 total, to your savings. Adding an additional sum each year certainly accounts for some of the $245,000 difference.

But the majority of the difference—approximately $180,000—is based solely on the power of time and compounding. You achieved a solid rate of return and allowed time to work in your favor. (Resulting in one of the few situations where time really is your friend.)

Establishing a Family Benchmark and taking steps to do everything you can to reach that benchmark is critical to reaching your goals. But you can't simply choose a high benchmark and assume everything will work out. If your goal is to save $100,000 in 20 years and you can only put aside $1,000 a year, you'll need a 14 percent annual rate of return to achieve your goal. That could be tough. Your Family Benchmark must be realistic.

Tie the Steps Together

Later you can see how you can strive for an achievable Family Benchmark. For now, let's bring the process full circle.

First you set your Balance and Base by establishing goals. You dreamed—and dreamed big.

Then you worked on Closing the Gap by analyzing your current situation. You assessed your financial position and your strengths and weaknesses. (If you're like most people, you probably spent a lot of time thinking about your weaknesses, and that's okay—each weakness is an opponent you can overcome.)

You know where you are, and you know where you want to go.

How do you get to where you want to go? You reach your goals through discipline, through experience, through following a smart financial strategy, and through your Family Benchmark.

So let's see how it works in action. Real life is extremely complicated; I'll keep things simple so the process is easy to follow. Along the way you will control what you can't control, and you'll adapt to situations you can't control—just like Brazilian Jiu-Jitsu.

Starting Point

Let's use a premise we can all relate to: Saving for retirement.

Keep in mind that this is a concept everyone can relate to, but also a concept I don't fully embrace. When I talk about "retirement" later in the book, you'll find out I don't believe in the traditional concept of retirement. Why work your whole life just so you can stop and sit? I don't ever plan to retire; I love what I do, I love working with people . . . so why would I want to suddenly stop? (And if I didn't love what I do, I would find something I do love—although it's a cliché, life is too short.) Sure, I may focus on other pursuits, I may spend more time on charitable or community efforts, or I may take my vocation in a completely different direction . . . but I will *never* retire. I plan on working—at the things I enjoy—until the day I die.

You should, too.

So for the sake of argument, let's say you plan to "retire" at a certain age; instead of working full time in your current job, you want to work in volunteer programs helping troubled youth. (If you choose to volunteer and help people in need, that's a full-time—and incredibly rewarding—job.)

In order to "retire," you decide you'll need a total of $800,000 in retirement savings. That number doesn't include Social Security or pensions; you feel you need $800,000 in your own retirement account. How did you arrive at that number? You took a look at your current lifestyle, thought about how you want to live, estimated your expenses, and decided you need $75,000 before taxes to live the way you want to live. Each year you'll draw $75,000 from your account; doing some quick math shows your account, if it continues to earn an 8 percent return, will last until you're 90 years old.

At that point you'll run out; if you think you'll live longer you could reduce the amount you draw each year. Again, we're keeping things simple, so let's assume you estimate a life expectancy you're comfortable with, and you're not concerned about leaving an estate. (I have a friend whose father likes to say to him, "Son, don't expect an inheritance. I plan to spend my last dollar on the day I die." We think his father is joking, but we're not sure.)

So you need $800,000. You're 30 years old and you plan to "retire" at age 67, which is the official Social Security retirement age for your date of birth. Anyone born from 1960 on is considered for Social Security purposes to have a "full retirement age" of 67. That gives you 37 years to reach your goal.

You make $40,000 a year. You've worked hard to cut down your expenses—you embrace the concept that the pain of discipline completely and totally outweighs the pain of regret—and you determine you can put $3,000, before taxes, away for retirement. As a bonus your employer offers a 50 percent match on retirement contributions (you'll learn about retirement funds and matching contributions later; for now just think of it as "free money," because in essence it is). So in total you will contribute $4,500 per year toward your ultimate goal of $800,000.

Now let's look at some possible scenarios. Two factors stay the same: You have 37 years to grow your account, and you will put $4,500 a year into that account. As a result, if your Family Benchmark is 0 percent and you earn no return on those savings:

	Annual Rate of Return	Total at age 67 (37 years)
$4,500 contribution per year	0%	$166,500

Obviously you are far short of your $800,000 goal. Let's look at another scenario using a 5 percent rate of return:

	Annual Rate of Return	Total at age 67 (37 years)
$4,500 contribution per year	5%	$480,200

Better . . . but you're still short. What if you are able to achieve an 8% rate of return?

	Annual Rate of Return	Total at age 67 (37 years)
$4,500 contribution per year	8%	$986,900

At a Family Benchmark of 8 percent you will reach your goal—and then some.

But life isn't always that simple. Markets are volatile. Some years investments do well, other years not as well. Only Ponzi schemers *promise* a predictably high return; trustworthy, reliable financial planners only pledge to do their best to help you reach your goals. To promise a high rate of return is to promise something that cannot be delivered.

So what happens if for a one- or two-year period your investments do not hit your Family Benchmark target in terms of return? What happens if for two straight years you earn no return? Even though long-term time is on your side, over the short term you do lose a little of the power of time and compounding. For example, say for the first five years you contribute $4,500 per year but you do not achieve any return on that investment; the rest of the 32-year period you do achieve your Family Benchmark of 8 percent. Here's what happens then:

	Rate of Return	Total
$4,500 contribution per year	0% (5 years)	$ 22,500
$4,500 contribution per year	8% (32 years)	652,300
Total balance (after 37 years)		**$674,800**

Now you're short. But that's okay; time is on your side. Although you didn't receive a return early on, you do have time to make adjustments and make up the difference. (How do I know you have time? Making adjustments and shifting priorities is one of the key ways I try to help my clients reach their goals. I constantly evaluate their investment performance with their short- and long-term goals, making adjustments all along the way.)

For example, you and your wealth advisor may have decided the best investments for you—based again on your goals and also on how much risk you are willing to accept—was a specific blend of stock and income-generating investments, diversifying your portfolio to mitigate some risk while maintaining flexibility so you can seize opportunities as they arise. The goal is to do everything possible, because there are no guarantees, to meet your Family Benchmark of an 8 percent return.

But now you're behind. You have a few options:

- You could decide to wait longer to start drawing from your retirement funds. If you wait until you are 70, for example, the power of time and compounding will increase your total savings to nearly $800,000.
- You could decide to contribute more to your retirement fund. If you increase your annual contribution from $4,500 to $5,000, you will wind up with $725,000 at age 67—much closer to your target. (To hit your $800,000 target you'll need to increase your total contribution, for all the 32 years remaining, to $5,500 per year.)

Or, you could revise your Family Benchmark. That could be a better strategy. Why?

First, you may not be able to wait until age 70 to start drawing retirement funds; Social Security may not exist, at least in its present fashion, and if you don't have another type of pension, you may need to start tapping your retirement savings.

Second, you may not be able to contribute more to your account each year. Some years you might, but what if you face an unexpected emergency? What if you're sick or injured for part of a year? One thing I can promise is that the unexpected will occur. Luke, my Brazilian Jiu-Jitsu instructor, likes to say that on the mat the unexpected is simply not possible because you should always expect *anything* to happen; if *everything* is expected then by definition *nothing* can be unexpected. The same will be true in your financial life; expenses will pop up. Creating a plan to reach goals that simply assumes, "I'll come up with more money to save if I need to," is a plan that is destined to fail. I can't instantly become stronger when I face a stronger opponent; you can't instantly find extra money to save when your investments don't perform as you hope.

That's why I help all of my clients establish a Family Benchmark, and that is why you should establish a Family Benchmark. Where are you starting from? Where are you going? Your Family Benchmark is the tool that will help get you from starting point to destination.

Otherwise you are just *hoping* things will turn out. Hope without discipline, without a plan, and without focused action is, well, just a dream.

Your Family Benchmark creates a framework and a mental approach designed to help you turn dreams into realities by allowing you to adapt to changing circumstances. Harness the power of time and compounding, and do everything possible to achieve the rates of return required.

Family Benchmark

Every journey contains a path, and your Family Benchmark is like a guide that ensures that you know exactly where you are on that path. Brazilian Jiu-Jitsu is based on maintaining control and staying flexible; your Family Benchmark can provide the security that comes from knowing your goals are achievable while allowing flexibility to respond in the face of changing circumstances. Best of all, your Family Benchmark is based on your goals for yourself and your family. If you know the "why" then the "how" becomes a lot easier.

- Consider your goals.
  Where do you want to go? Start with the end in mind.

- Consider your current position.
  What can you contribute to reach your goals?
- Establish a Family Benchmark.
  Given your position, what will it take to reach your goals?
- Constantly reevaluate.
  Track your progress, track your results, and adapt to new circumstances as you follow the Way2Wealth.

Does reaching your goals seem like an impossible task? It may be—if you go it alone.

Almost no one is able to accomplish anything worthwhile on his or her own. Why even try when there are people who can help you? Let's build a team to help and support you on your Way2Wealth.

CHAPTER 5

Your Team of Advisors

TWO IS BETTER THAN ONE:
THE POWER OF RESPECT

Mark DellaGrotte has trained fighters including Kenny Florian, Frank Mir, and Patrick Côté. He once told me, "Before a fight, watch the fighter's trainer. Is his fighter nervous? Does the trainer look like he's been here before? Does he trust his fighter? Does he trust himself?" *I watch corners all the time now; you can tell a lot about how the fight will go before it even begins. If the captain of the ship doesn't know what he's doing it doesn't bode well for his fighter.*

—Sam Sheridan

At the age of 55 the average client has three advisors. At the age of 60 the average client has one advisor. At some point people realize they need to work with an advisor who puts together a personal investment plan as opposed to a general investment plan. Find the advisor, as soon as you can, who will help you navigate the rest of your life based on your needs and your goals.

—Jim Lake

One of my favorite stories has little to do with financial planning and building wealth, and everything to do with the way I feel about my profession. I'll let my friend Tom Hine tell it,

> Years ago I met with a client to review his portfolio. As he sat down I noticed he didn't look like he felt well. I asked him how he was doing and he said he didn't feel great.
>
> The next time we met we had a mini-celebration because his portfolio was doing very well. He was a little subdued, though, and finally told me, "I've got some bad news. I just met with a new doctor; turns out my old doctor missed the warning signs. I have cancer."
>
> At that moment his portfolio, his wealth, and his investments meant nothing to him. What really mattered was his health. I realized then my job isn't just to help my clients invest well; I'm really doing my job when I care about each person in all aspects of their lives. That moment really crystallized my thinking about how to focus my practice. I still help my clients make money, but now I focus even more on the total picture: their health, their well-being, and what they want to achieve in life. A good wealth advisor doesn't just care about helping clients make money; he or she cares about caring.

If you ever wondered what separates a good wealth advisor from a great wealth advisor, now you know the answer.

We care. Not just about numbers, but about you as an individual.

The same is true in Brazilian Jiu-Jitsu. Take it from one of the best teachers, my friend Renzo Gracie:

> My job is to bring out the best in each person. I get more joy from helping a guy in need than from helping to build a champion. I get real joy out of helping an insecure person become more confident. Confidence is the main tool in life. Brazilian Jui-Jitsu and martial arts in general make you a better, more confident person. As a teacher, what more could you ask for?

So how do you find someone to help you reach your goals? How do you find a great wealth advisor? To answer that question, let's start by looking at the different types of advisors available.

Types of Advisors

Before I hit the mat and start rolling with different types of professional advisors, let's get one thing straight: Many people are smarter than I am, especially in their fields. That's why:

- If I want to buy property, I talk to a real estate broker.
- If I'm about to sign a contract, I see my lawyer.
- If I get too badly banged up on the mat, I see (reluctantly) my doctor.

That's why I go to the Clinch Academy to train in Brazilian Jiu-Jitsu: Luke, along with many of the guys there, knows much more than I do. I'm never too proud to admit I need help; I think admitting that I need help is a strength, not a weakness. (In fact, one of the greatest weaknesses is failing to admit when I need help.)

I know a lot about investing, about wealth management, about financial planning . . . I've worked and studied and exposed myself to as many opportunities to learn as I could find. But that doesn't mean I know everything about everything; far from it. I'm okay with that; I turn to people who can help me. I would much rather ask for help than make a mistake. I would much rather seek guidance from someone who has knowledge and experience.

I would much rather succeed by seeking help than fail on my own.

Let's look at some people who can help you succeed; all you have to do is let them. Professionals can help you with:

Investment Advice   "Financial Planning" is a term often used in the financial services field. Financial planning is a broad term and can cover many different types of financial professionals. In general, though, a financial planner helps you invest your money. (Many can help you put a household budget together as well, but now you know how to do that on your own. Budgeting doesn't require expertise, but good budgeting does require discipline.) Some financial planners are better than others—better qualifications, better track record, and so forth. Good wealth advisors get to know you, learn about your goals, your dreams, your needs, your current situation—and develop investment plans taking into account all those variables. In order to reach your dreams and hit your Family Benchmark, a good wealth advisor is absolutely crucial.

Estate Planning   Depending on the nature of your family and the extent of your assets, estate planning can get extremely complicated. (Trust me when I say it's not as simple as writing a will.) Estate planners specialize in helping you minimize the effect of taxes, maximize the amount of money and assets you can pass on to your heirs, and just as important help you make sure your wishes are carried out when you pass away. Tax laws change constantly, especially where estate planning is concerned. Most experts recommend reviewing and possibly revising an estate plan every two to three years.

Here's an unpleasant example of an unexpected consequence where an incomplete estate plan is concerned. Say you are divorced and have a child. If you are single and you don't have a will (which makes you like at least 30 percent of Americans under the age of 40) and you pass away, your assets and property go to your child.

So far so good.

But say you remarry and you don't create a will, much less a more comprehensive estate plan. If you die unexpectedly (is there any other way to pass away?), your assets and property goes to your new spouse.

Your child is legally entitled to—you guessed it—nothing. But if you bequeath certain assets to your children in a will, he or she will receive what you want your child to receive.

That's why a good estate planning professional does more than, for example, help your heirs avoid estate taxes. Good estate planners can help you foresee and avoid situations you may never have considered. Otherwise if you pass away what happens is based on what the law requires, which may not dovetail with what you would wish.

Who knows better what you want? You? Or the government? I think you do—but you have to take steps to make sure that what you want will actually happen.

Tax Planning If you're new to investing and don't have much in the way of assets, tax planning will likely be reserved to making sure you take the deductions you are entitled to when you file your income taxes. Later, tax planning can play a critical role in preserving and growing your assets. A good wealth advisor can help you implement investment strategies that minimize taxes and maximize your earnings—and will let you know when outside help makes sense. (For example, I provide my clients with tax-planning services as a part of my total wealth-planning process.) In investment terms, good wealth advisors understand the tax ramifications and strategies necessary to maximize your overall returns; in other aspects of your financial life, consulting with an accountant may be necessary.

Insurance I talk about insurance later, especially life insurance and how it fits into your overall financial plan. Insurance is another specialty; insurance agents can help you determine the coverage you need under terms you can afford.

Quick note In the past some people turned—and I guess in some cases still do—to "retirement planners" for help when they retired, under the assumption they had special needs that only a retirement specialist could meet. I no longer feel that's true or necessary. When people are young, they typically are more willing to take on risk. When they retire, many people shift their investments into vehicles that tend to carry less risk in order to safeguard their nest egg. A good wealth advisor can take you from cradle to grave, in effect: Although your needs certainly do change, understanding and then helping to meet the ever-changing needs of a diverse client base is what a good wealth advisor does best.

In short, if you find a great wealth advisor, stick with him or her for the long run. Great advisors—and great teachers—are able to adapt to the needs of their clients and students.

All Those Initials: Professional Designations

Professionals working in the financial services field tend to have many initials after their names. I'm no different, although for the most part I try to keep my initials to myself: I'm an RFC (Registered Financial Consultant), a member of the Financial Planning Association, and a Paladin Registry Advisor.

The initials can be important, though. Let's take a quick look at what some of the designations and certifications mean. Just keep in mind that a designation or certification is not a guarantee of skill or a particular level of service; what it does mean is that the person has met the requirements to achieve certification. Just like earning a college diploma doesn't automatically make someone smart, earning designations and certifications doesn't guarantee skill. (But it is one factor you can take into consideration.)

> **Certified Financial Planner (CFP)** A CFP has met the requirements to demonstrate a level of competency in a fairly broad range of financial-planning skills. The qualification program involves learning about stocks, bonds, taxes, insurance, retirement planning, and estate planning. A number of exams are given along the way, plus a tough final exam. Designees must have experience in financial planning and agree to meet a code of ethics and professional responsibility that the CFP board enforces. You can check with the CFP board at any time to find out if a certified professional is in good standing.

Registered Financial Consultant (RFC) This designation is awarded by the International Association of Registered Financial Consultants to members who have met education, experience, and membership requirements, have agreed to abide by a code of ethics, undertake 40 hours of continuing education each year, and fulfill many other qualifications.

Certified Public Accountant (CPA) CPAs are like accountants with black belts; they have a degree in accounting, have passed the CPA exam (no mean feat in itself), and have demonstrated experience in the field. A CPA can also become a Personal Financial Specialist (PFS) by having three years' experience in financial planning and—you probably saw this coming—passing a rigorous exam.

Chartered Life Underwriter (CLU) CLUs tend to work in the insurance field; qualifying requires three years' experience and demonstrated proficiency in a variety of different aspects of insurance: life and health insurance, pension planning, insurance law, income taxation, investments, financial and estate planning, and group benefits. How do they demonstrate proficiency? No surprise: CLUs take 10 different courses and sit for about 20 hours of exams.

Again, initials are important—but many other things matter, too. It works the same way in Brazilian Jiu-Jitsu and in the martial arts in general. Most martial arts award belts to students who meet the qualifications for that belt; as you advance through the ranks the qualifications get tougher and tougher to meet. In some cases those qualifications are largely based on time; in other cases the qualifications are largely based on demonstrated ability.

But regardless of how belts are conferred, a belt is not a guarantee of skill. Having a black belt in karate does not guarantee that you can defeat any green belt. A Brazilian Jiu-Jitsu brown belt can never count on tapping out every blue belt who walks in the door. Belts are indications of skill and proficiency, not guarantees. Certifications and designations are indications of proficiency, not guarantees.

Think of certifications and designations as indications, not guarantees. Take additional steps to find the right individuals to work in your corner. How?

In a little bit I walk through the steps you should take in finding the right advisors for you. Before I do, I think it's helpful to understand how financial advisors are compensated.

How Financial Professionals Earn Their Keep

In some cases it's easy to understand how professionals are compensated. Lawyers, for example, tend to charge by the hour, although some will charge by the "project." For example, a lawyer may quote a set fee to perform a title search and to represent you at a real estate closing. In most cases lawyers charge by the hour simply because they cannot accurately predict how much time a particular matter may take; charging hourly helps them ensure that they do not over- or undercharge clients while still being fairly compensated for their services.

Understanding how other professionals are compensated can be trickier. Take insurance agents; if you purchase a life insurance policy, the agent's fee comes out of the total premium you pay. (You have no way of knowing the amount of that fee; all you know is the total of your premium.) In some cases the agent's fee is "front-loaded": he or she gets a major portion of the first one or two premiums, and then the percentage drops over time. (That's one of the reasons why insurance agents work hard to land new clients.) In some ways it is not important to know how much the agent is paid: If you shop around, thoroughly understand the components and conditions of the policy, and feel the price is competitive, that should really be all you are concerned with.

Professionals in the financial services industry are compensated differently. Some work on commission only, some work for a fee, and some are paid by a combination of commission and fee. Let's look at each compensation method:

Fee-Based Compensation   A fee-based financial professional charges a fee for services rendered. Some advisors perform an assessment of your situation and your goals, and deliver a comprehensive plan to help you meet those goals. In return you are charged a fee (a fee you should know up front). After that you may choose to work with another professional, like an investment advisor, to implement that plan. Or you may continue to work with the original professional, paying an hourly fee for any services rendered. In effect, fee-based advisors work similarly to lawyers; services are provided either for a flat fee or based on an hourly rate.

Some firms and professionals charge a fee based on assets under management. For example, if you have investments totaling $1,000,000 and your wealth advisor manages those assets for you, the firm may charge a percentage fee to manage those assets; those fees typically range from 1 to 2 percent per year or more. Early on you probably don't need to worry about "assets under management" fees, because those tend to only apply to high net-worth individuals. (But someday you might . . .)

Commission-Based Compensation   Commission-based financial professionals are compensated much like real estate agents; they are only paid as the result of a specific transaction or service. For example, if you purchase stock through a stockbroker, the broker is paid a commission on the transaction; the commission could be a flat rate per transaction or per unit of stock, or could be a percentage of the dollar amount of the transaction. In theory any advice, guidance, or consultations you receive are "free," although that time is built into the commissions the professional receives.

Combo Compensation   Okay, that's my term for this pay practice. Some advisors provide certain services for a fee, and others are based on commission. (This arrangement is common in the financial guidance field.) For example, your advisor may charge a flat fee to analyze your situation and develop a comprehensive wealth plan. The end result is a plan you can implement yourself, work with another advisor to implement, or work with the initial advisor to put into practice. If you stay with the initial advisor, he or she will then work on a fee or commission for services provided. I think it's a great compensation model. Once the plan is in place, clients are only charged for services rendered, resulting in a win-win outcome for client and advisor.

Which type of compensation arrangement should you choose? There are no hard and fast rules. The key is to know what you will receive for the fee or commission you are charged; if you get value for your money, how you are charged is not important.

But what's important is making sure that you thoroughly understand, up front, how and when you will be charged for any services rendered.

Choosing an Advisor

You understand the initials, and you understand how advisors earn their keep . . . so what's next? It's time to pull the pieces together and select the right advisor for you.

Let's start with a basic premise. One way to think about wealth advisors is to think about where organizations like the Ultimate Fighting Championship (UFC) started. The basic premise of "ultimate fighting" was to answer a simple question: In martial arts terms, what really works in real-life situations? Boxing? Karate? Wrestling? Other martial arts?

What really works?

The answer surprised everyone. Renzo Gracie, weighing in at a comparatively small 180 pounds, beat a number of larger fighters from a variety of disciplines. At first few could believe what they saw: How could this little guy cause larger fighters to submit? The answer was that ground-fighting skills are incredibly important in real-world situations, because most fights end up on the ground . . . and Renzo's Brazilian Jiu-Jitsu skills made all the difference.

That's how I found Luke and the Clinch Academy. A friend I trust referred me to Luke.

It works the same way in the financial world—and in any other professional or business settings. Designations and certifications are great, and are certainly importantly . . . but what matters most is what works. What has the advisor *done?* That's what really matters. Just like that, in the financial world it's great to have designations and certifications . . . but how have they done? So when you look for a wealth advisor, ask friends, colleagues, and other financial or legal professionals whom they would recommend.

Then, when you find a great wealth advisor, you'll have found someone who can help put the rest of your team in place. Find someone you trust, and they can help you pull together a great team.

So let's start looking!

Defining the qualities that make up a great financial professional could take up an entire book. (Don't worry—that's not where I'm headed.) Ensuring you find the right advisor boils down to a few simple principles. I was reminded of that when I spoke to Renzo Gracie recently. Renzo, in addition to being world-renowned in Brazilian Jiu-Jitsu and a respected Mixed Martial Arts (MMA) fighter, also runs a string of successful training facilities, including one in Manhattan. As a result he trains a wide variety of individuals, all the way from teenagers to in one case a sheikh. His New York location naturally draws a number of Wall Street professionals, and he shared this story with me:

> A couple of years ago a new student scheduled a private lesson. He walked in wearing an expensive suit. I told him to hurry and change. He said, "No, I just want to talk for an hour."
>
> We sat down and he said, "I just took a new job and I want to talk about how to deal with pressure. There can't be any bigger pressure than walking into an arena with 65,000 people watching you. How do I deal with that? And how do I establish myself with new clients? I feel a ton of pressure to generate clients; if I don't I won't have a job."
>
> I told him, "A lot of things are out of your control. You can't control certain situations. Since you work in an environment

that you as a specialist can do better than anybody else, and the situation can *still* get out of your control, the most important thing is that people can trust you. Take me. I would only feel comfortable giving you money to manage for me if I could reach you when I needed to and ask you questions. That way even if my investments don't do well, I will still want to work with you because I can communicate with you and I can trust you. I know there are ups and downs, but I want to know you'll be there for me no matter what. Be someone people can trust."

A year later he came in with a magazine in his hands; he was ranked number two in trustworthiness. Later he was promoted and moved up to a much higher position.

Jiu-Jitsu teaches you that you will face problems. Problems are part of life. Business and investing are the same way. Problems come and go . . . but trust can last forever.

I admire Renzo; he may be the nicest tough guy I've ever met. And he's right: Open communication and trust form the foundation of not just an advisor-client relationship but any relationship.

Let's go down the list of qualities that are critical. A good wealth advisor:

- Asks about *your goals* first.
- Spends time with you and listens to what you have to say.
- Offers more than one solution, and describes the pros and cons of those solutions in terms you can understand.
- Answers your questions when you don't understand.
- Is up front and open about his or her fees and compensation.
- Discusses the risks involved with any investment.
- Never pressures you to make a decision or reach an agreement.
- Tells you what you need to hear instead of what you might want to hear.

The last quality is incredibly important. A wealth advisor is paid to provide expertise. An advisor unwilling to—gently and kindly, of course—offer a different opinion or to disagree with you is not doing his or her job. My job, for example, is to help you reach your goals. If I simply go along with anything you say so you will "like me," am I really helping you reach your goals?

I don't think so.

Just make sure that an advisor who disagrees does so respectfully, thoroughly explains why, and helps you understand his or her point of view and reasoning. I don't have all the answers. You don't have all the answers. Together we have a much better chance of succeeding than we do individually. The best advisor-client relationships are collaborations: We listen, we ask questions, we explain, we adapt . . . we work hard to do our best for *you*.

That's what you want from your advisors.

Keep in mind the first quality on the list—asking about your goals right from the outset—is also incredibly important. As I like to say, don't bother caring about how much an advisor knows until you know how much the advisor cares.

Why? Think about it in Brazilian Jiu-Jitsu terms. If a potential student walks into the Clinch Academy, what is the first question Luke asks?

I know the answer: He says, "How can we help you? What can we help you achieve?" Luke is, first and foremost, an instructor and mentor . . . but he cannot teach someone unless he first knows what they want to learn. I realize the obvious answer may be as simple as, "Brazilian Jiu-Jitsu." But some students want to learn a new sport. Others want to get in shape. Still others hope to fight professionally. Different goals require different approaches, and Luke cannot tailor his approach until he first understands each student's goals.

To do that, he has to ask.

So does a wealth advisor. If a prospective advisor starts the conversation by listing all the services he or she can provide, that's certainly helpful . . . but where do *you* fit in? Where do *your* goals fit in? The best advisors ask about your needs and goals first, and then explain how they may be able to help you meet those needs and goals—and if they can't, they gladly refer you to someone who can.

Interview!

That's right. The next step is interviewing potential advisors. After all, they will work for you—shouldn't you make sure you want to "hire" them?

If you still feel uncomfortable with the idea of interviewing an advisor, think of it this way. If you need a loan, you probably are a little nervous when you walk in the bank. After all, the bank has to "approve" you, and sometimes that can feel like the bank is doing you a favor.

Stop thinking that way. The bank isn't doing you a favor. The bank *needs* you. The bank is in the business of lending money, and it needs customers. Without customers it has no business.

You may need a loan, but the bank needs customers like you in order to sell their products, which in this case is making loans.

The same relationship applies where wealth advisors are concerned. Although *you* need help and guidance, the *advisor* needs clients like you in order to make a living. An advisor without a client isn't an advisor; he's unemployed.

Or think about it in Brazilian Jiu-Jitsu terms. If you're unfamiliar with the sport and walk into a gym, you'll see some people on their backs. Are they in a disadvantageous position? Not necessarily; in grappling, the guard is actually considered to be an advantageous position because the fighter on the bottom can attack by using a variety of joint locks and chokes, while the primary goal of the person on top—aside from protecting himself—is to move into a more dominant position. (Which we call passing the guard.)

So let's assume the guard position and maintain control; no advisors will pass the guard while you're on the mat. What questions should you ask a potential advisor?

Stick with the basics:

- **Can you tell me about mistakes you've made over the year?** If the advisor can't share mistakes, that's a huge red flag. Everyone makes mistakes. What did the advisor learn? How did they overcome mistakes?

- **Can you give me examples of your experience and track record?** Most advisors will naturally try to provide positive examples, but what's important is to find out *how* they answer the question as well as the actual answer. For example, an advisor who tries to gloss over the question, or says, "Well, that's confidential," may not be the best choice for you. Advisors should be able to give you a feel for their track record. They could combine all their investors' results and provide an overall number; they could tell you about situations they handled well and situations they handled poorly but learned from . . . the key is to get a feel for how honest and forthright you feel the advisor answers the question. No advisor is perfect; good advisors readily admit that.
- **Can you provide references?** Again, some clients may say that information is confidential. But it shouldn't be; some clients should be willing to share their experiences (especially if those experiences are positive). Talk to current or past clients. See what they say.
- **What is your background?** Ask about certifications and designations. Ask what types of clients they have worked with in the past. Ask what types of clients they like to work with and feel they service best. Ask if they have ever declined to work with a client, and why.
- **What companies are you affiliated with? How did you choose those companies?** Advisors align themselves with a variety of financial service providers; knowing what criteria they or their firms used to select those providers is important information.
- **How many clients do you currently have? How much in terms of total assets does that represent?** Although an advisor managing a high dollar value of assets may not be a great advisor—after all, he or she may just have great connections—managing significant assets is a sign of success. But it could also mean your portfolio—and you—could get lost in the shuffle. So finish with:
- **What can I expect from you? How often will you call? How often will we speak? How quickly do you return calls? How**

will you work with me? Again, understanding expectations is critical. Your advisor provides a service; know what that service entails.

- **How are you paid?** The best relationships are open and honest, and knowing how you will be charged is critical. The advisor might be paid a commission on the securities or investment vehicles he or she sells. The advisor may charge a fee, either as a flat fee or as a percentage of the assets they manage on your behalf. The advisor may work on an hourly rate basis. Or, most likely, the advisor uses a combination of these compensation techniques depending on the services rendered. Your goal is to understand precisely how the arrangement will work. Make sure you understand the requirements and conditions right up front; that way there will be no misunderstandings later.

And one other thing: If a wealth advisor feels she is not the right fit for your needs, she will happily send you on your way so you can find a better match for your situation, goals, and interests.

Also don't be afraid to trust your instincts. When I first met Luke, I knew he was the right Brazilian Jiu-Jitsu instructor for me, and nothing has happened to change my mind. (In fact, I'm even surer now than I was then.)

When you meet with a wealth advisor for the first time, what do you notice first? You might see a fancy office filled with diplomas and certificates, but what you should notice right away is whether you hit it off and feel comfortable. Your goal is to develop a long-term, lasting business relationship with your wealth advisor. Do you want to work with someone you don't enjoy spending time with or even talking to?

I wouldn't. Life is too short. Although you don't need your wealth advisor to be your friend, you do want him or her to be *friendly*. There's a big difference.

Most importantly, keep this in mind:

When you look for a wealth advisor, you don't care about how much the advisor knows until you know how much the advisor cares.

Take the time to find out if your advisor will care about you as an individual. I'll take an advisor who cares about me over a knowledgeable but uncaring and disengaged advisor any day.

Trust—But Verify

One last comment about advisors: The last thing you want to do is to turn your wealth plan—and the responsibility for your financial future—over to your advisor. Don't be passive. Don't just watch. Work closely with your advisor. Ask questions. Ask for advice. Continue to adapt and develop plans that meet your needs and your goals. If you start to feel the relationship is not as solid as it once was, don't be afraid to say so—and don't be afraid to take your business elsewhere.

It's your money. It's your family's future—treat it as the precious commodity it is.

Two Is Better Than One: The Power of Respect

Know what you know; know what you don't know. Be open to advice and guidance. Respect the power of teamwork and collaboration. No fighter steps on the mat alone . . . not really. Coaches, teachers, instructors . . . they are all in his corner.

In the best relationships, clients and advisors act as equals. In reality, asking for help doesn't give away control. Instead, letting others guide you and help you allows you to be more successful than you could ever be on your own.

In Brazilian Jiu-Jitsu, going to your back often means you gain control—even though others might think you've lost all control. When you ask for help, the same thing occurs: You may appear to give up control, but when you get good advice you actually gain more control over your financial future.

- Understand which advisors you need.
  Assess your goals and your current situation, and look for help.
- Understand the compensation structure.
  Understand what you will receive—and what you will pay for.

(Continued)

- Interview candidates—after all, you're "hiring" them! Relationships are based on communication
- Focus on credentials and "desk-side manner" to find the right advisors for your specific needs.
  Life is too short; work with people you enjoy and trust.
- Get advice—but stay in the guard position.
  Ask questions, stay in touch, and stay on top of your money.

Try to find someone who can put the whole team of advisors together; not only will that ease your burden but will also help ensure that your team works well together. If a great wealth advisor pulls together the rest of the team, he will find people who will collaborate to ensure that your best interests are always served. Don't look for a collection of individuals; work to create a team.

I can't say this strongly enough: Your future, and your family's future, is too important. Never go it alone. With a little effort you can build a great team for your corner. And once your team is in place, you're ready to start rolling and take concrete steps toward reaching your goals.

To this point I have focused on training and preparation; now it's time to hit the mat and start investing!

CHAPTER 6

Timing

WHAT IS YOUR INVESTMENT STRATEGY?

Buy quality. Buy good funds, invest in good stocks, and work with good wealth managers. My outlook is pretty simple: Find quality people, quality companies, quality boards of directors . . . think quality all the way through. Quality always pays off.

—Ron Carson

There are no shortcuts if you want to succeed long-term. Nothing replaces having the discipline and putting in the time and the effort to develop into a great Jiu-Jitsu player. Personal finance works the same way. Trying to make a lot of money in a short period of time almost never pays off. Trying to hit home runs means you'll probably strike out. Hit singles and doubles and you'll score a lot of runs over the long term. Nothing—in Jiu-Jitsu or in building wealth—happens overnight.

—Jeff Rozovics

Everyone's investment strategy is different. That's a good thing: We all have unique needs and goals. Our plans and strategies should be unique.

But at the same time, most investment strategies do include a few common elements. Think of those common elements as some of the basic holds and techniques in Brazilian Jiu-Jitsu. Some advanced techniques don't work for everyone. Each person brings a different level of flexibility, strength, and speed to the mat, so certain holds and moves work better for some people than for others. But all of us need to know how to pass a guard, to establish side control, to apply basic locks and submission holds.

So where do you start? I assume you are new to investing, and I start with the basics. Each stage along the way forms a building block on the Way2Wealth—so don't skip steps!

Stage 1: Build an Emergency Fund

Credit cards are not emergency funds, even though many people think they are.

I understand why. After all, if you have a credit card with $1,000 in available credit and you face an emergency, you can tap that card to cover an unexpected expense.

Although that approach makes sense, it's also a recipe for long-term financial problems. Since you can't afford to pay off the balance right away—because if you could pay off the balance you would simply have used cash instead of credit—each month you pay interest on the outstanding balance. Over time the $1,000 you spent turns out to be much more when interest charges are figured in . . . and if you have another emergency, then where will you turn?

A true emergency fund is cash, not credit. Everyone needs a little money put aside to cover unexpected expenses; if you don't, that's the first place to start.

You might never have to touch the money. That's great, because your emergency fund can earn interest and grow along with your other investments. But if you do need to tap into your emergency fund, you will have access to money you won't have to borrow.

How much do you need? Many financial experts feel the average person should just pick a number: Some say $500, others

$1,000, others $2,000. Another approach is simply to keep three to six months' worth of salary in an emergency fund.

Either approach is too simplistic. The Way2Wealth is based on flexibility and each person's individual situation, needs, and goals. Let's take the time to calculate how much you need in your emergency fund.

Determine Your Target

Keep in mind that your emergency fund should only be used for true emergencies like medical expenses, car repairs, home repairs ... spending outside your control that you must have cash in order to cover. Repairing the car that gets you to work is an emergency; coming up with cash because your favorite store is running a major sale is not an emergency.

The key is to think about your individual situation and the options you might have. Do you have two cars? Do you and your spouse both work close to home? If that's the case and one car breaks down, you might be able to wait a week or two to get it fixed. If you end up in the hospital, in most cases the hospital won't expect payment immediately, which gives you time to develop other options for making payment.

So think back to the last real emergency you faced. How much money did you have to spend? More importantly, how much money did you *need* to spend? That number is a start ... but let's take the process farther by reviewing five tips:

1. **Pull out your Expenses Worksheet from Chapter 3**. The amount you spend each month is the amount you need to live exactly as you live at this moment. That's a great starting point, but if you lost your job, would you still spend the same amount each month? Probably not—you would cut back wherever possible.
2. **Evaluate your expenses.** Which expenses can you eliminate or reduce? If you had no income, could you cut down on entertainment? Could you cut back on meals, cable, clothing, and so on? Go through your expenses, line by line, and eliminate or reduce any spending you can. When you're done, the

only expenses left should be true essentials like mortgage or rent payments, utility payments, and food. You don't have to maintain your fitness club membership, but you do have to feed your family.

3. **Determine your new total.** Add up all your "have to" expenses; that's what you need in order to live for a month.

4. **Step back and think.** You did cut expenses to the bone, but could you live with what you decided? Can you really see yourself cutting out your child's dance lessons? If the cuts you made seem too extreme, look at a few different scenarios. You can certainly add expenses back in—just be sure to understand that the more expenses you include on your list the larger the emergency fund you'll need. In the end your plan needs to be a plan that you can maintain in real life, not just on paper.

5. **Multiply by six.** If you face a major emergency, like the loss of a job, you may well need six months' expenses to get by, especially if you have a family. (If you're single and have no kids, you may be able to get by on three months' worth of expenses.) If you're unsure, shoot for six months. If you put that much aside in your emergency fund and later decide you could do with less, you can always shift some of that money into other investments. Either way the money in your emergency fund is money saved—not money borrowed or spent.

Table 6.1 is a quick example using three months' of expenses as a target; keep in mind that I've left a lot of expense categories out to make it simple:

Table 6.1 Emergency Fund Worksheet

Type of Expense	Current Expense	Emergency Reduction
Mortgage payment	$1,200	$1,200
Car payment	300	300
Utilities	175	175
Cable	95	40

Table 6.1 (*Continued*)

Type of Expense	Current Expense	Emergency Reduction
Food	600	450
Entertainment	200	50
Clothing	100	20
Total	**$2,670**	**$2,235**
Months		3
Total Emergency Fund		**$6,705**

I realize that the thought of having $6,000 or more in an emergency fund may sound like a lot; the key is to see your emergency fund as a target to build toward. The beauty of your emergency fund is that it cannot just be a "savings account" but also part of your overall investment strategy, because you can get a return on the money in your emergency fund. So in no way is your emergency fund a waste of money. You might never need to tap it. If you don't, you'll earn a return on the investment; if you do, you can cover unexpected expenses without taking on debt.

Win-win!

Take a moment and complete your own Emergency Fund Worksheet; the resulting number is your target.

Emergency Fund Worksheet

Type of Expense	Current Expense	Emergency Reduction
_____	_____	_____
_____	_____	_____
_____	_____	_____
_____	_____	_____
_____	_____	_____
_____	_____	_____
_____	_____	_____
_____	_____	_____

(*Continued*)

Emergency Fund Worksheet (Continued)

_____	_____	_____
_____	_____	_____
_____	_____	_____
_____	_____	_____
_____	_____	_____
_____	_____	_____

Total $_____

Months Required (circle)   3   4   5   6

Emergency Fund Target $_____

Stage 2: Own Your Home

Even in down markets, real estate investments tend to be good long-term investments. That premise is especially true where owning your own home is concerned. Why? You have to live somewhere, and renting a residence means someone else is paying off her mortgage and taking advantage of the tax benefits and potential appreciation of the property; so shouldn't you be enjoying those benefits and not your landlord?

Appreciation

As recent trends show, there is no guarantee that home values will rise, especially in any short-term period. But over the long term home values have tended to rise, making a home purchase a solid investment.

Of course, unless you're incredibly driven to build wealth, other considerations play a part when you choose a residence besides the potential to make a profit. If you have a family, you want a home in a good neighborhood and a good school district. Quality of life is important.

But that's okay: Homes in good neighborhoods and good school districts that provide a solid quality of life tend to be more valuable. They also tend to grow in value faster because people want to move into desirable neighborhoods.

Tax Benefits

The tax benefits of owning your own residence are considerable. If you rent, you cannot claim your rent payments as an itemized deduction on your income taxes. If you own a home, the interest portion of your mortgage payment is tax-deductible and reduces your income tax burden.

Say your monthly house payment is $1,000 and approximately $950 of that is interest; at the end of the year you can deduct $11,400 from your adjusted gross income. (If you have only had your mortgage for a few years, the amount of interest you pay is relatively high because almost all of your payment in the first few years goes to paying off interest charges rather than paying down principal.)

If you are a renter and pay $1,200 per month, the $14,400 you pay each year for rent cannot be deducted from your taxes.

Again, although every individual situation is different, the average person can safely assume that he can save approximately 15 percent to 20 percent of the monthly mortgage payment in taxes. (An accountant or tax professional can help you determine exactly what you can save based on your individual financial situation.) As a result, if you pay $10,000 per year in interest you can probably assume your tax burden will drop by $1,500 to $2,000 each year. Effectively that means you only paid $8,000 to $8,500 in house payments, not $10,000.

And there is another bonus to home ownership—if you sell the home, you will probably not have to pay capital gains tax on any profit you make. If you live in a home for two years and sell it for a $30,000 profit, you will not owe any tax on that profit as long as you purchase another home within six months of selling the previous home. You can use this real estate capital gains exemption over and over; as long as you buy another home, you can "upgrade" into larger and more expensive homes without paying capital gains tax.

If you currently rent, work hard to put yourself in a position to own your own home. You'll feel a real sense of pride in ownership, and you'll enjoy financial benefits, too.

Another win-win!

Stage 3: Take Advantage of Tax-Deferred Investments

If you are an employee and you are not taking advantage of your company's 401(k) plan, you are missing a tremendous opportunity. For example, if you are currently under 30 and you start saving today, you could easily have between $1 and $2 million in retirement savings by the time you are in your mid-sixties.

Here's why. Contributing to a 401(k) plan results in:

- A lower taxable income, which reduces the amount paid in taxes each year.
- Automatic savings and earnings because your contribution is automatically deducted from your paycheck (remember one of my core principles, Make it Automatic?).
- Additional contributions by your employer (if your employer provides a match).
- A better opportunity to retire on your terms and at a lifestyle you hope to live.

Even people in their fifties can take advantage of the power of a 401(k) plan. They won't enjoy as much of the power of compounding, but they will enjoy the other benefits of tax-deferred savings.

That's why contributing to a 401(k) plan is Stage 3 in your investment plan; I can think of no logical reason not to contribute if a plan is available, especially if your employer provides a match to your contributions. (I discuss the employer match later.)

401(k) Plans: The Basics

Do you need to know the ins and outs of 401(k) plans? Probably not . . . but knowledge is power, so let's make sure you're operating at full power.

A 401(k) plan is considered to be a "defined contribution plan." Other defined contribution plans include profit-sharing plans and Individual Retirement Accounts (IRAs). Each is called a defined contribution plan because the amount that is contributed is defined either by the employee (that's you)—or the employer.

Four things make a 401(k) plan different from other retirement plans:

1. **When you participate in a 401(k) plan, you decide** how much money you want to contribute. Under normal circumstances you can contribute as much as 15 percent of your gross pay, but your employer does have the right to limit the total amount you contribute. (Few do, though.)
2. **The money you contribute comes out of your check** before you're taxed and before you can spend it. (Make it Automatic!) A 401(k) plan is probably the easiest way to save for your retirement because it is automatic. And in effect you pay less tax each pay period, and each year, because your income is "lower."
3. **Many employers match a portion of your contribution.** The matched amount is basically free money—it's like your employer's gift to you (as long as you participate in the plan, of course).
4. **Your money is held by a third-party investment firm** and not by your employer. Your money is safe even if your employer goes out of business. You also get to choose how your money is invested; the investment firm handling the fund normally provides a number of options. (I talk more about some of those options later.)

The bottom line: You are in charge, your income taxes are lower, your employer may give you what amounts to free money, and your investments are protected even if your company goes out of business.

What's not to love about a 401(k) plan?

There is one potential aspect that might be less than lovable: The only negative side effect of contributing to a 401(k) plan occurs when you withdraw your money before you reach age 59½. If you do, you will be required to pay taxes on the amount you withdraw as well as a 10 percent penalty to the IRS. But that's okay because if you really need the money you can typically borrow against your 401(k)—you'll see how in a little bit. (You won't face a penalty or tax liability as long as you pay that loan back.)

Tax Advantages

Why are you better off contributing to a 401(k) plan than simply investing in, say, the stock market?

It's a common question based on the nature of 401(k) plans: If you simply buy stock in the open markets, you are not penalized when you sell those stocks.

There are a number of reasons a 401(k) is a better plan than making your own investments. (Of course, that doesn't mean you shouldn't do both types of investing; remember, we're at Stage 3.)

The main advantages to a 401(k) plan are that the money is contributed *before* it is taxed and your employer may match your contribution. There are other advantages, too, but let's talk about the two main advantages first.

Pretax Investing   A quick math example shows the advantage of pretax saving.

For example, say you decide you will have $100 deducted from your pay each month and placed in your 401(k). Let's assume that before you started your 401(k) your gross pay was $3,000 a month and your net pay was $2,160. You paid $840 in taxes because you are in the 28 percent tax bracket. (I'm keeping the math simple.)

Because the $100 for your 401(k) comes out of your pay *before* payroll taxes are calculated, you are in actuality only taxed on $2,900 in gross income. As a result you pay $812 in taxes, making your take-home pay $2,088, $72 less than before you started your 401(k). So although you contributed $100 to your 401(k), it only "cost" you $72. You saved $28 per month on the $100 you put toward your retirement.

Along with reducing the income taxes on your salary you also will not have to pay any tax on money your account earns—until you start making withdrawals when you retire. At that point most people find themselves in a lower tax bracket, so the tax bite they face is typically lower. In the meantime your 401(k) grows, tax-free.

Free Money   We all know nothing is free, don't we? In this case that's not true.

Although not required by law, many employers match at least a percentage of what its employees contribute to their 401(k) plans. A match is a way for the employer to offer an employment benefit and help people like you create a retirement plan of your own (especially since many employers no longer offer company-funded pensions).

Say your employer offers a 50 percent match on your contributions. (Many offer 100 percent, but only up to a certain limit.) If you contribute $100 per month, like in our earlier example, your employer will contribute $50. Each month your account grows by $150, not $100, even though you only chipped in $100 of that $150. Excluding any earnings on the investment, at the end of the year you will have at least $1,800 in your account instead of $1,200. (That's why the employer match is free money.) And you won't pay taxes on the employer match, either.

There are limits. Some employers will match up to 3 percent, or 5 percent, or whatever specific percentage they choose. Employers are under no obligation or requirement to match any contributions, but again, many do.

If your employer offers a match, do everything possible to contribute enough money to get the maximum match available. If your employer matches 100 percent of your contributions up to 3 percent of your pay, for example, contribute enough to get that amount. (If you make $30,000 a year, 3 percent is $900, meaning your employer will give you $900 . . . for free!) If you aren't in a position to afford the contribution necessary to max out your max today, work hard to make it possible as soon as you can.

If you aren't taking advantage of matching contributions, you're leaving money on the table. If your employer offered you, for example, $2,000 extra a year, wouldn't you grab it?

Stage 4: Max Out 401(k) Match Contributions

Even if you wanted to, federal guidelines do not allow you to contribute an unlimited amount to a 401(k) plan. Typically the cap is 15 percent of your salary, although special conditions sometimes do apply.

To keep things simple, I assume that you can only contribute up to 15 percent of your pay. Initially you may not be able to afford to contribute the maximum allowable into your 401(k). But, in general terms, that should be your goal.

A wealth advisor can help you determine whether maxing out your 401(k) contributions makes sense for you; my goal is to give you general, not specific, advice.

If maxing out your 401(k) contributions sounds a little over the top, let's look at a few scenarios. (If you want to play around with different retirement savings scenarios, use an online financial calculator designed to model how much your retirement account will be worth based on different contribution amounts, earnings, and time periods. To find one, search for "retirement calculator" or "401(k) calculator.")

For example, say you are now 30 years old and you plan to retire at age 65. (Of course your "official" retirement age will be 67, but you may decide to retire earlier.) You currently earn $40,000 a year, and you plan to contribute 5 percent of your pay. Your employer will match 50 percent of your contribution. To keep the math simple, I assume that your Family Benchmark is 7 percent, meaning you want to average a 7 percent return on your investments.

Under the above conditions, and assuming that you never receive a pay increase, when you retire you will have $430,273 in your account.

Sound good?

Let's take it a step farther. Say you commit to saving 7 percent of your pay under the same terms. When you retire, you'll have $573,691, or over $140,000 more—simply by contributing 2 percent more of your pay, or $800 per year.

Sound better?

Now let's go to the extreme. Say you put 15 percent of your pay into your 401(k). Your employer will only match up to 6 percent of your pay, but that's okay because you are still getting free money. When you retire you will have $1,032,654 in your account!

Actually, you'll probably have much more than that, because your income will increase over the years and your contributions will automatically increase, too.

That's why you should be as aggressive as you can when you fund your 401(k). The money you spend at lunch today will be forgotten tomorrow—but someday your retirement savings will mean the world to you.

If You Can't Max Out Today

What if you can't max out your contributions to your 401(k) plan today? Here are a few tips to get you there:

- When you receive a pay increase, increase your contribution percentage immediately. If you get a 3 percent raise, increase your contribution by 3 percent. Chances are you won't "feel" it.
- If you pay off a long-term debt, raise your contribution. Say you have a car payment of $300 a month and you make $40,000 a year in salary. Three hundred dollars per month is $3,600 per year, which is 9 percent of your gross pay. When you pay off the car, your expenses are lower; put an additional 5 percent to 7 percent of your pay into your 401(k), and you can still spend the same amount on all your other expenses.
- If you find ways to cut other monthly expenses, allocate the amount you save toward your 401(k). Money you no longer have to spend should become money you save, especially when your employer will kick in free money, too.

The best thing about a 401(k), other than the tax advantages and the employer match, is that the money is deducted from your pay automatically. It's hard to miss what you don't have.

What if your employer does not offer a 401(k) plan or a 401(k) plan is otherwise not available to you? Or what if you have managed to max out your 401(k) plan contributions?

Stage 5: Contribute to Traditional and Roth IRAs

Individual Retirement Accounts (IRAs) are another form of tax-deferred investment. Sometimes people use the terms 401(k) and IRA interchangeably, but they are completely separate investment vehicles, even though they do share some similarities. Mixed martial arts and Brazilian Jiu-Jitsu are completely different forms of fighting, although they do share similarities.

The key is to know the differences and understand how those differences can help you.

As with 401(k) plans, let's start with the basics. There are two main types of IRAs that most people can contribute to: traditional IRA and the Roth IRA.

Which is better?

Neither . . . and both.

Confused? Don't worry; I'll clear up any confusion.

Traditional IRA

A traditional IRA is a tax-deferred retirement investment similar to a 401(k). The difference is that anyone can contribute to an IRA, even if he is self-employed and therefore is not offered a 401(k) plan by an employer.

On the other hand, a person enrolled in a 401(k) plan can also contribute to an IRA.

Like a 401(k), contributions are made on a pretax basis. As a result, you lower your current income taxes, and your money grows tax-free until it is withdrawn. You can, if you choose, start withdrawing at age 59½. but you must start making withdrawals when you reach age 70½.

Advantages of a Traditional IRA   The tax savings at the time of investment are considerable, and could even put you into a lower tax bracket. Plus, your income is likely to be lower when you retire, so you'll make withdrawals at a lower rate. And, your money grows in value tax-free while it's in the IRA.

Disadvantages of a Traditional IRA   Eventually you'll have to start withdrawing funds whether you want to or not (once you reach the age limit), and you will be taxed on those withdrawals.

Roth IRA

A Roth IRA is a tax-*exempt*, not a tax-*deferred*, retirement investment vehicle. *Contributions* to a Roth IRA are not tax-deductible when they are made but *withdrawals* during retirement years are tax-free. You can start withdrawing at age 59 ½, and you are not required to make any withdrawals at any age if you choose not to.

Confused? The difference is actually fairly simple. When you contribute to a traditional IRA, you contribute money before income taxes are taken out, as you do with a 401(k). When you take withdrawals at retirement, those funds are taxed at that time. (That's why a traditional IRA is tax-deferred.) When you contribute to a Roth IRA, you contribute money after taxes are taken out; if you like, think of it as writing a check out of your take-home pay, not your gross pay. But, when you take withdrawals at retirement, you aren't taxed on those withdrawals—not on the money you originally contributed and not on any earnings you have received over the years. That's why a Roth IRA is tax-exempt; once the money is in the account, you don't pay taxes when you withdraw it.

Advantages of a Roth IRA   The biggest advantage of a Roth IRA is that withdrawals are tax-free on both principal and earnings. If your account grows in value by hundreds of thousands of dollars, you won't pay taxes on that growth when you withdraw your money.

Disadvantages of a Roth IRA   You may not qualify if your income is too high, and you won't receive any tax benefits when you actually put money into the account.

Which Is Better?

Both a traditional IRA and a Roth IRA are great investment and retirement savings options. You really can't go wrong investing your money in either type of IRA. But I can give you some general advice, depending on your situation:

- If you are already funding a 401(k) plan, you are already enjoying some benefit from tax-deferred investing. In that case you may decide to fund a Roth IRA before a traditional IRA; that way you can build a blend of tax-deferred and tax-exempt investments.
- If you are not able to contribute to a 401(k) plan because your employer doesn't provide one, consider putting some money in a traditional IRA and some in a Roth IRA (assuming you can't fully fund both). Again, that way you can build a blend of investments.
- The younger you are, the more strongly you should consider funding a Roth IRA. The longer the time period before you retire, the greater the power of compounding—the more your earnings grow, the more you'll enjoy tax-free withdrawals.

401(k) and Roth

Let's take a common scenario to show you how this could work. Say you can't afford to make a maximum 401(k) contribution or a maximum Roth IRA contribution—what should you do?

If your employer matches part of your 401(k) contribution, then your 401(k) is your best form of saving. Say, for example, your employer matches 50 percent of the first 6 percent you put into your retirement plan. In that case, putting funds in your 401(k) provides you with an instant, guaranteed 50 percent return on your money. You put in $10 and your employer adds $5. There simply is no better and more immediate investment return.

Once your 401(k) is fully funded up to your employer match, you might consider adding any additional funds you have available to a Roth IRA, especially if you're relatively young. Over the years, the time value of your money will cause it to grow exponentially, and you won't pay taxes when you start to withdraw it.

The bottom line:

Although you should always consult with a financial professional who can consider your individual circumstances, here are some basic guidelines:

- If your employer offers a 401(k) plan, max it out, at the very least up to the amount your employer will match.
- If your employer doesn't offer a 401(k) plan, max out a traditional IRA first and then a Roth IRA, or consider investing a portion of your savings into each type.

Getting Started

So how do you contribute to an IRA? You'll need to set up a plan with a financial services firm. It's easy; call a financial services provider, talk to an advisor, and ask for information on IRAs. Feel free to give me a call; I can steer you in the right direction.

Then find out:

- **Where your money will be invested.** Some banks will only allow you to invest in a Certificate of Deposit; financial services firms tend to offer a full range of investments just like with 401(k) plans.
- **Fees required?** Some firms charge a fee to open an account or to make deposits to an account; others do not.
- **Deposit options.** Direct deposit is a great way to fund IRA accounts. (Make it Automatic!)
- **Transfer fees.** If you decide to transfer your account to another firm, some firms charge a fee; most do not. Make sure you know what is involved, just in case.
- **Investment changes.** Some firms will ask you to change your investment allocations as frequently as once a day; others only allow you to change weekly or monthly.

Then compare your options and choose the firm that provides the best combination of fees and services.

Stage 6: Determine How to Invest Your Funds

A great aspect of 401(k) plans and IRAs (as well as many other investment vehicles) is that you get to make choices about where your money is invested. When you contribute to an IRA or 401(k), you get to choose how to invest that money. Everyone has different goals, and your investment choices should reflect your individual goals. Think about your Family Benchmark; what are your goals?

Deciding how to reach those goals can get incredibly complicated, though. As you develop as an investor you can invest in the stock market, commodities, foreign currency, gold and silver . . . so let's keep it simple; as you learn more and as you gain more experience, you may decide to explore other investment opportunities. But for now let's focus on your 401(k) and your IRA investments. How should you invest those funds?

I'll answer that question after providing a little background information.

The typical 401(k) plan may offer 20, 30, or even more investment choices, including:

- Stock mutual funds
- Bond mutual funds
- Stable value accounts
- Money market accounts
- Endless combinations of the choices above

You choose where to place your money. You can put the entire balance into one category or type of fund, or divide your money across different funds or investment types.

What are the differences in the investment vehicles listed above? How should you invest your money to get the best return and still be relatively safe if the market swings dramatically? Unless you work with a wealth advisor, in most cases your plan administrator (the investment company that handles the accounts) won't advise you on exactly where to invest, other than by providing some generic guidelines.

Let's take a brief look at the categories listed earlier:

Stock mutual funds are portfolios of stocks. When you buy a share of stock, you purchase a small share of ownership in the company. A stock mutual fund buys shares of stock in a variety of companies with the goal of getting a solid return on those investments. The price of a share of a mutual fund is based on the value of all the stocks it owns at any given time. When those shares increase in value, so does the mutual fund share price. Since mutual funds tend to own hundreds of different stocks, no one stock can cause the share price to rise or fall dramatically.

Think of a stock mutual fund as a way to have a professional manager invest your money for you.

Bond mutual funds are like stock mutual funds except they invest in corporate or municipal bonds. A bond is like an IOU—you purchase the bond, and a company or government promises to pay you back, with interest. Bond mutual funds typically focus on purchasing high-yielding bonds. In general a bond mutual fund is somewhat less risky than a stock mutual fund . . . but certainly not always.

Stable value accounts and **money market accounts** typically consist of certificates of deposit (CDs) and U.S. Treasury securities like Treasury Bills. These funds are generally secure, but on the flip side offer small and steady growth. You won't get rich overnight, but your money should be relatively safe.

So how should you invest your 401(k) and IRA accounts? The key is to determine your goals and evaluate your willingness to take a risk.

How much risk you're willing to accept is an extremely important consideration.

You can take a conservative route and invest in stable value funds, which will generate lower returns but also create a lower probability of loss.

- Or you can take a middle-of-the-road approach and invest in a combination of aggressive and conservative options; you'll tend to face a little more risk in the hopes of receiving a somewhat higher return.
- Or, you can be a little more aggressive and select funds with higher earning potential but that naturally come with somewhat higher risk. Typically as a fund's potential return increases, its level of risk increases.

The possible combinations are almost endless. Every fund carries risk, so one general rule of thumb is that the longer you can keep your money in an IRA or 401(k) (in other words, the longer until you plan retire) the more risk you can typically take on with the goal of seeking higher returns. For example, if you think you'll need the money sooner rather than later, your willingness to take on risk is likely to be lower, causing you to choose investments with a fairly consistent and stable history of returns, like bond funds or stable value funds.

If you have many years of investing ahead of you (say at least 10 to 15 or more), then you can probably afford to take more risks, because the longer your money is invested the more time you have to recover from short-term losses.

Your own feelings about investing are also a major consideration. Spending sleepless nights worrying about your investments is no fun at all. (I know; my firm has hundreds of millions of dollars in assets under advisement. I worry about my money and my clients' money.) Think about how much risk you are comfortable with, consider your Family Benchmark, and then plan your investments accordingly.

And keep in mind that most plans let you rearrange your funds a number of times each year—in many cases as often as you want—so if you change your mind you can also make changes to your investments. Your investment decisions won't be set in stone.

A Closer Look at 401(k) and IRA Investment Options

Let's dig a little deeper into the choices available to you.

Stock funds Of all the choices available, stock funds are typically the riskiest but also the ones with the most earning potential. Historically, stocks as a whole have enjoyed an average annual return of more than 10 percent. Some years less, obviously, and some years more . . . but over the long term the return has averaged a little more than 10 percent.

The tricky part is to select the right stock mutual funds. How do you know which are the best-performing funds?

Index funds According to a number of investment professionals, index funds tend to be the best-performing type of stock fund. An index fund is designed to, in large part, "match" the performance of the stock market. Index funds consist of representative amounts of each stock in the Index. For example, a Standard & Poor's 500 index fund is made up of a blend of all the stocks in the Standard & Poor's 500. Index funds have been, in the past, the safest way to get a steady return on your investment—assuming, of course, that the future will be similar to the past. (And there is no guarantee of that.)

If your plan doesn't include an index fund, chances are good it does include a fund that is similar to an index fund.

Growth funds Growth funds buy stocks the fund managers feel are likely to grow in value. Within this category you'll often find subcategories like:

Aggressive growth funds, which focus on riskier but potentially high-return stocks.

Moderate growth funds, which combine a blend of risky and less risky stocks.

Value funds, which concentrate on relatively stable stocks that often pay a dividend.

There may be other subcategories as well; your plan should describe the goals and level of risk in each.

Small-, medium-, and large-cap funds Stock funds are often categorized based on the size of the companies they invest in, which is called market capitalization. The market cap of a company doesn't refer to the size of the company (like number of employees, locations, facilities), but instead to the stock market value of the company. The market cap is calculated by multiplying the number of shares outstanding by the price of those shares. The result is the market capitalization value.

Small-cap funds   typically invest in companies with a market value of less than $1 billion. Small-cap funds can at times yield high returns but are also considered by many to be relatively risky.

Mid-cap funds   invest in companies with a value ranging from $1 billion to around $8 billion to $10 billion. Mid-cap funds tend to be less risky than small-cap funds but also tend to produce lower returns over time.

Large-cap funds   invest in companies with market values over $10 billion. Large cap funds often function similarly to an index fund by investing in all of the companies in that particular index. Large-cap funds tend to carry less risk but at the same time generally provide a relatively lower return on investment.

Sector funds   invest in companies in a particular industry, like pharmaceuticals, or health care, or technology, or gas and oil companies. If you feel a particular industry is poised to take off, sector funds can be a great way to participate in their financial success without facing the risk of only buying, for example, one oil stock.

International funds   invest in stock from countries around the world.

Income funds   invest in stocks that pay a regular dividend, or in bonds, or in a variety of combinations. The goal of the fund is to minimize risk while maintaining a reasonable—although typically small—return on investment.

Life-cycle funds   create a blend of stocks and other investments based on your age and desires. The goal is to create a blend of funds that matches your level of risk and hoped-for rate of return. For example, your 401(k) may offer:

Conservative, Balanced, Growth, and Aggressive allocation funds. Each attempts to perform like its name.

"Destination 2015," "Destination 2025," "Destination 2035" funds While these types of funds may have different names, the goal of this type of fund is to spread investments appropriately based on when you hope to retire. For example, a Destination 2025 fund is intended for a person who wishes to retire in the year 2025.

Confused? Don't be. The beauty of a 401(k) or IRA is that you don't have to choose any one fund. You can spread your investments across different funds to try to maximize your returns and hit your Family Benchmark while you take on only the amount of risk you wish to face.

If you're new to investing, it makes sense to start with a more conservative approach. As you learn more about the stock market, the bond market, and investing in general, you can consider taking on more risk. Over time you'll develop a feel for your level of risk and how you wish to invest your money.

Another approach, of course, is to get advice from a wealth advisor. That is what I recommend; it's our job to keep up with the markets, with the economy . . . and to care about you and your investments. Investing wisely is a full-time job; if you already have a full-time job, do you want to take on an additional job? Learn all you can . . . but also enjoy the power of your team. Don't go it alone—your money and your family's future is too important.

Investing by Age

Interested in taking a different approach? Here's a guide you can use to determine how to allocate your investments. Go to your age category and check out some general guidance:

Age 20 to 29 You're relatively young, you're establishing your career, and you probably have less disposable income than you would like.

Here's how you might consider allocating your investments:

Index stock fund	50%
Small-cap stock fund	25%
International stock fund	25%

Age 30 to 39   You're still young, have probably started a family, and you probably own a home. (If you don't, please work hard to buy your own home—why pay rent?)

Here's how you might consider allocating your investments:

Index stock fund	50%
Small-cap stock fund	15%
Mid-cap stock fund	15%
International stock fund	20%

Age 40 to 49   You are probably doing well financially, at least in terms of day-to-day cash flow, but thoughts of having enough money to retire comfortably may worry you.

Here's how you might consider allocating your investments:

Index stock fund	40%
Small-cap stock fund	15%
Mid-cap stock fund	15%
International stock fund	15%
Bond fund	15%

Age 50 to 59   You're nearing "retirement," are at the peak of your earning power, and you're still concerned about whether you have enough money to retire the way you'd like.

Here's how you might consider allocating your investments:

Index stock fund	30%
Small-cap stock fund	10%
Mid-cap stock fund	20%
International stock fund	10%
Bond fund	30%

Keep in mind the above allocation percentages are only guidelines; use the percentages as a starting point for your own decisions. Make sure you always adjust your plans to fit your financial situation, Family Benchmark, and willingness to take on risk.

Stage 7: Diversify into Other Investments

If you are fully funding a 401(k), taking advantage of traditional and Roth IRAs, and have more money you can invest, make sure that those funds work just as hard for you.

The same principles apply to other investments as they do to retirement savings. You can invest in the same type of funds, such as income funds, mutual funds, and index funds, but to do so you will need to open an account with a wealth advisor.

Keep in mind that becoming a great—meaning successful—investor takes a lot of time and effort. If you go it alone, you'll need to stay focused on your investments and stay up-to-date on economic trends and other factors that affect your investments. If you're up for the challenge, there are tons of classes, books, seminars, and other products designed to help you learn more about a seemingly endless variety of investment strategies.

The odds are good, though, that for most people taking the time and putting in the effort to become a sophisticated investor doesn't make sense. You already have a full-time job and in all likelihood a family. Are you willing to spend the time necessary to learn the skills required to succeed in what, if you think about it, is another career?

You probably don't—and that's okay. A skilled wealth advisor can guide you on the path to wealth, and help you learn what you need to know to better manage your investments; together you can form a great team and make great decisions.

If you're a brand-new investor, get a wealth advisor to help you. Then when you gain knowledge and experience, you can take a bigger role in making decisions. I turned to a great teacher to help me learn Brazilian Jiu-Jitsu. I could have read a few books and done it alone . . . but I would be nowhere near as skilled as I am now. Learn from the best—and take advantage of the skills that the best have to offer.

But no matter what, start investing today.

Take it from my friend Jim Lake, National Sales Manager of Guardian Annuities and a Brazilian Jiu-Jitsu purple belt:

> Invest early, invest often. What is the right time to invest? The right time to invest is when you have money. Don't wait. Don't procrastinate. Invest now.
>
> And invest for the long run. If you don't wait, and pay yourself first, over the long run you will build wealth. Take $100 today and set it aside. Create a plan and put money aside every week, every month, and every year. Take the first step, get off the sidelines, and start investing. You'll be amazed how easy it is. Trust your advisors. Trust the system. That's what successful investors do – and that's what successful Brazilian Jiu-Jitsu fighters do. We trust the system.
>
> But no matter what you do, get off the sidelines. You have to be in the game to have a chance at winning.

I couldn't have said it better myself.

What Is Your Investment Strategy? Timing

Don't wait. Start investing now so you can begin to build a great financial future. You can't grow assets unless you have assets; you can't grow wealth unless you have money to invest.

And don't go it alone. Find a wealth advisor to help you. Great wealth advisors can offer advice and guidance it would take you years to learn. You already know your goals and your Family Benchmark. You have a great sense of where you're starting from—now leverage your knowledge to build a plan to get where you want to be.

Investing to grow wealth is a lot like learning new skills in Brazilian Jiu-Jitsu. The more you know and the more you invest, the more options and strategies you have at your disposal.

- Build an emergency fund.
  Decide how much you need and take steps to create a cushion
      for when the unexpected occurs.
- Own your own home.
  Don't pay rent if you don't have to; when you do, you pay
      someone else's mortgage . . . and give them the opportunity
      to take advantage of tax breaks and appreciation.
- Take advantage of tax-deferred investments.
  Contribute to a 401(k), contribute to traditional or Roth IRAs, and
      take advantage of the power of tax-deferred and tax-
      exempt investing.
- Invest your funds according to your goals and your Family
  Benchmark.
  Choose investments that fit your individual needs.
- Diversify into other investments.
  But don't go it alone; take advantage of the skills and guidance
      of others.
Use your team!

The key is to develop a plan—and stick to your plan. Building wealth takes time and concentrated effort. Make it automatic, save and invest consistently, and trust your wealth advisor to help you make good investment decisions.

And while your wealth is growing, so is your estate—so let's put some plans in place to make sure your hard-earned money benefits your family, now and forever!

CHAPTER 7

Gain Control

YOUR ESTATE PLAN

The most common mistake I see is people failing to have even the most basic estate plan. People come to me who are worth hundreds of thousands of dollars . . . and they don't even have a basic Will. (Or if they do, it was created twenty years ago and is well out of date.) Estate planning beats investment planning every time. As a wealth advisor I can never help clients make enough money to cover mistakes they make in their estate plan. Don't focus on the front end—like setting up complicated investments—until you take care of the back end—your estate plan.

—Ron Carson

My goal at the Clinch Academy is to create a sense of family—a family that will outlive me and our current members. By that I don't mean a family-friendly atmosphere, although that is important. I mean a sense of excellence, of history, and of tradition . . . I hope to pass on my knowledge, my skills, and my ethics to others, and I hope they do the same. All of us will leave behind a lot more than money—to the people who love and respect us, our values, ethics, and history is what matters most.

—Luke Rinehart

If you die tomorrow, what will happen? What happens to your assets? What happens to your family? What happens to your children? Don't assume "it will all work out." It will—but it may not "work out" the way you want or would intend. An estate plan ensures your wishes and your desires are carried out; if you don't have an estate plan, you leave the outcome to chance . . . or to government guidelines.

Who knows what is best for your family?

Of course—you know what's best for them. So don't leave them hanging. Estate plans are not complicated to set up, and even if they were, they would still be worth doing. What is more important than your family's well-being? Isn't their future worth a little effort, especially if you won't be there to help them?

Again, creating an estate plan is relatively easy. We'll work through the basic steps. Keep in mind that if you are single, don't have any kids, and don't have much in the way of assets you may not need every item in an estate plan—but as your life gets more complicated, your estate plan should become more comprehensive as a result. Establish what you need now, and add to your plan down the road.

Estate Plans: The Basics

Some situations are easier to think about than others. Planning for your death—or for a serious illness or injury—may not sound like much fun, but if you don't create an effective estate plan, you'll add legal problems, confusion, and stress to the emotional turmoil your family will naturally experience. In Brazilian Jiu-Jitsu terms, failing to create an estate plan is like failing to establish yourself in the guard position if you're on your back—not only have you given up control, but you've made a potentially bad situation a whole lot worse.

Keep in mind that many people assume an estate plan is something wealthy people need so they can help their families avoid estate taxes. Although minimizing the tax burden is certainly a benefit of an estate plan, there are a number of other benefits as well. A good estate plan:

- Provides financial stability for your spouse, children, or other beneficiaries.
- Protects your assets for future generations to enjoy.
- Ensures your wishes are carried out.
- Protects your loved ones' privacy.

Estate planning lets you determine who receives your assets, determines how and when those assets are distributed, and determines who can act on your behalf and for your benefit in case you are incapacitated or face a major medical emergency. If you don't have an estate plan, all those decisions could instead be made by a court, by inheritance laws, or by health-care professionals.

Sound gloomy? It doesn't have to be. Seven basic documents will cover most situations for the average person, regardless of how high—or low—his or her net worth.

The tools you will probably need include:

- Revocable Living Trust
- Pourover Will
- Health-Care Power of Attorney
- HIPAA Power of Attorney
- Property Power of Attorney
- Family Retirement Preservation Trust
- Estate Planning Letter

They may sound complicated and a little intimidating, but they're not. Let's take a closer look at each of the items in a comprehensive estate plan.

Revocable Living Trust

The Revocable Living Trust is a versatile and effective estate-planning tool. Unlike a will, a trust avoids the publicity, delay, and expense of probate.

Here's why. A will is a legal document that takes effect after the creator of the will passes away. If you create a will, you specify who will inherit your assets and what they will receive. When you die, your will enters a legal process called "probate," where the will is "activated" and the executor, or person you specified to carry out your wishes, is granted permission to act on your behalf.

Wills are public records; when you pass away, anyone is allowed to view your will. That's how people find out what celebrities did with their estates; journalists—and anyone else—can readily see a will. While you're alive, the will is private; once you die and the will enters probate, it is fair game for anyone to see.

Wills that are properly drafted can work their way through probate fairly quickly; a poorly drafted will could sit in probate for a long time.

In the meantime your assets sit, too.

That doesn't happen with a trust. A Revocable Living Trust, (meaning a trust you can modify or even dissolve), can:

- Take care of your short- and long-term financial and health-care needs if you are disabled or incapacitated.
- Eliminate or reduce estate taxes.
- Provide tremendous control over the disposition of your assets. For example, if you have children from a previous marriage, you can ensure that those children get what you want them to receive; if you don't have a trust or a will, your assets pass to your current wife—not to your children.
- Avoid guardianship or conservatorship if you are incapacitated. (In short, help keep others from making decisions if you are no longer able.)
- Reduce the threat of contestation. Wills are often contested, especially if relatives feel they do not receive their "fair share" of the estate. In most states, your trust is allowed to include a "no-contest" clause, which can deter challenges to your estate plan.
- Protect your heirs from creditors. Assets that have been placed in the trust cannot be seized in divorce or bankruptcy proceedings.

- Control your assets after you're gone. If you have young children, you can control the assets they receive until they are old enough to take responsibility for themselves.

That's a lot of advantages from a relatively simple document; so how does a Revocable Living Trust work? First you set up and then transfer assets to the trust. You are named as the Trustee and Beneficiary of the Trust, so you remain in complete control. You can receive income from the trust, sell assets, acquire new assets . . . you can make any decisions you want. And, you can amend or even revoke your trust at any time.

In effect, placing assets in a Revocable Living Trust is nearly the same as owning your property directly—except when you die.

Once you die, because legally the trust was the owner of your assets, there is no reason for probate to take place. Assets in the trust are simply distributed according to your instructions. Your Successor Trustee (the person you selected to carry out your wishes) is required to follow the instructions you left behind. And unlike a will, which is a public document, all the details of your trust remain private, do not require any court approval, and do not create additional expense for your estate.

A Revocable Living Trust is a powerful and versatile tool. A qualified estate-planning attorney can help you set up a trust that delivers the greatest benefit to you and your family and takes into account both your family's needs and the laws in your state. (Every state has its own set of estate-related laws.)

Pourover Will

A Pourover Will is like a safety net for your estate. If you forget to transfer assets into your Revocable Living Trust, when you die, a Pourover Will automatically transfers those assets into the trust. Pourover Wills can also distribute tangible personal items like furniture, jewelry, clothing, or other personal property.

A Pourover Will is fairly simple, and has only one beneficiary: Your Revocable Living Trust. The Pourover Will transfers assets to the trust so those assets will be subject to the trust's distribution plan—*your* distribution plan—and can receive the benefit of your trust's tax reduction provisions as well.

Think of it this way. Say you set up a Revocable Living Trust this year. Ten years from now you haven't updated the trust, added assets, made changes . . . and your wealth has grown considerably. If you have a Revocable Living Trust but don't have a Pourover Will, you could end up with two distribution plans: The assets controlled by your trust will be distributed according to your instructions . . . and any assets not controlled by your trust will be distributed based on the inheritance laws of your state.

A Pourover Will keeps that from happening.

Health-Care Power of Attorney

A Health Care Power of Attorney allows you to appoint another individual to make health-care decisions for you. If you are incapable of making health-care decisions due to illness, injury, or incapacitation, your designee has the power to make decisions for you. Health-Care Powers of Attorney can be amended or revoked at any time as long as you are considered competent.

Unlike a Living Will, which typically only addresses situations involving life-sustaining medical treatment, a Health-Care Power of Attorney can cover a broad range of health-care decisions and is not limited to instances of terminal illness or permanent coma. The Health-Care Power of Attorney is a comprehensive and flexible document. The person you choose is authorized to weigh the facts and legally speak for you according to guidelines you provided.

Because your agent is authorized to make decisions on your behalf, it's important that she understand fully what your wishes may be under different circumstances. Choose a person whom you trust and with whom you feel confident discussing your intentions for medical care. It is more flexible than a Living Will, so the Health-Care Power of Attorney is a useful document that can spare you and your family pain and heartache. Your agent does not need to agree with your wishes, but must respect your right to receive the kind of treatment you want.

HIPAA Power of Attorney

The Health Insurance Portability and Accountability Act (HIPAA) regulates how health-care providers are allowed to share your personal health information. HIPAA regulations were designed to protect your privacy and confidentiality. A Health-Care Power of Attorney gives your designee authority to make medical decisions for you if you are unable to do so. But, because of the penalties involved, some health-care providers may be reluctant to share medical information with your designee. Because the person you appointed may need to make decisions on your behalf during a medical crisis, it is critical that he or she have immediate access to information about your condition, your prognosis, and potential treatment plans.

An estate-planning attorney will ensure your HIPAA Power of Attorney contains specific language allowing your designee to receive personal health information in accordance with all HIPAA regulations, so he or she can act according to your intentions.

Property Power of Attorney

A Power of Attorney gives a person, typically called an "agent" or "attorney in fact," the legal authority to act on your behalf. Unlike a Health-Care Power of Attorney, which covers medical situations, a Property Power of Attorney allows you to choose who will act on your behalf in financial or business situations.

Property Powers of Attorney are extremely flexible: You can limit your designee's authority to a specific situation, like closing on the sale of a home or signing a specific contract, or give him or her authority over a broad range of situations or circumstances. A Power of Attorney can be temporary or permanent, can take effect only if you are incapacitated, and can be revoked at any time.

A Property Power of Attorney is an effective way to protect your interests if you become disabled or incapacitated, because your agent can step in to handle all or part of your business or personal affairs. If you do not have a Property Power of Attorney and are unable to manage your affairs, a court may appoint a guardian or guardians to act on your behalf—often without your input or agreement. A Power of Attorney allows you to choose, ahead of time, who can act for you and under what circumstances, limits, and guidelines.

Family Retirement Preservation Trust

This one is a little more complicated, but because the average person has a significant sum invested in retirement accounts, it can be an important estate-planning tool.

After you reach the age of 70½ you are required to begin withdrawing assets held in your 401(k) or IRA. The percentage you must withdraw each year increases over the remaining years of your life. So far so good . . .

But if you die and leave your 401(k) or traditional IRA to your children (or other beneficiary) that money is taxable when it is withdrawn. (Note this doesn't apply to a Roth IRA, which passes as tax-exempt "income.")

Creating a Family Retirement Preservation Trust allows you to pass on retirement assets to younger beneficiaries so they can stretch the income tax deferral over their longer life expectancy. Because the trust is the beneficiary of your IRA or 401(k), your beneficiaries are not required to immediately withdraw funds.

In fact, you can keep younger beneficiaries from taking control of those assets before you wish them to, simply by making that clear in the trust.

The Family Retirement Preservation Trust also qualifies as what lawyers often call a "Conduit Trust." A Conduit Trust allows you to ignore what is called a remainder beneficiary, or a person or organization that will receive your assets if the primary beneficiary is no longer alive. If your remainder beneficiary is an older person or is a charity, without a Family Retirement Preservation Trust they won't be able to stretch out the minimum required distributions to maximize the benefits of tax deferral—benefits you worked so hard to create.

If you don't plan to withdraw all of your 401(k) or IRA assets before you die, creating a Family Retirement Preservation Trust allows you to get the maximum "stretch" for distributions and softens the tax bite on your retirement plans.

Estate Planning Letter

An Estate Planning Letter is one tool that doesn't require the help of a lawyer. An Estate Planning Letter designates who will receive your tangible personal property like furniture, jewelry, collectibles, and family heirlooms. An Estate Planning Letter cannot be used to control cash, securities, real estate, and any objects that are not tangible and personal. In fact, an Estate Planning Letter is allowed in most but not all states, so make a quick call to an experienced estate-planning attorney where you live.

Unlike a will or a trust, an Estate Planning Letter only needs to be signed and dated to be valid. And you can create a new letter at any time, without seeing your attorney.

Plus, they are easy to write. Simply list each item of personal property and designate the beneficiary. Make sure you describe each item clearly to avoid confusion or contention after you die.

When you're done, you'll have a comprehensive and effective plan that protects your assets, helps minimize taxes . . . but most importantly provides for your family and ensures your wishes are carried out. As Ron Carson says: Take care of the back end first—no amount of planning on the front end can overcome a failure to create an effective Estate Plan.

But Don't Simply File Your Plan Away!

When your plan is set up, you probably will walk out of your lawyer's office and breathe a big sigh of relief. A comprehensive estate plan protects your assets and plans for your family's future.

Creating a trust is only the first step in the estate planning process, though.

The next step is to periodically review your estate plan to make sure it accurately reflects your *current* goals and requirements. Chances are your personal and financial situation will change over the years.

Why would you need to review your estate plan? Over time, at least one of the following situations may apply:

- **Change in marital status** Although your marriage marks a wonderful change in your personal life, marriage does not automatically change your will or trust and will not necessarily adequately provide for your new spouse. Marriage does give each spouse some rights to the other's property, but you should change your plan to ensure it reflects any new goals, both individually and as a couple. If you and your new spouse both have children from a previous marriage or relationship, revising your estate plan is essential to make sure you properly navigate the complexities involved in providing for children of blended families.

- **Divorce** During your marriage, your estate most likely provided for your spouse. After a divorce that goal is likely to change—so should your estate plan. Once your divorce is finalized your estate plan should be revised as quickly as possible to reflect any new goals and desires.

- **Additions to the family** If you don't have children your estate plan is probably set up to distribute your assets to your surviving spouse, to your parents, or to a charity or civic organization. Once you have a child, you'll probably want your son or daughter to be a recipient of at least some portion of your assets. And you may want, in addition to providing for your child's financial future, to appoint a legal guardian for your child in the event you and your spouse die or are incapacitated. (Otherwise the state may take over.)

- **Your family faces illness or injury** If you or one of your family members becomes seriously ill or injured, you may want to consider changing your estate plan to reflect their increased needs. For example, if a child has special needs, you can leave assets in a Special Needs Trust that will not disqualify him or her from receiving government benefits. Or you may wish to shift the distribution of assets to help provide for his or her increased financial requirements.

- **You simply change your mind** Over time goals and wishes naturally change. You may decide to select a different Trustee or agent for your estate. You may wish to distribute assets differently. You may decide to include your grandchildren in your estate plan. The possibilities are endless. Your estate plan should reflect your *current* intentions, not the intentions you had 5 or 10 years ago.
- **Tax laws change** Changes in tax law can dramatically affect what happens to your estate. For example, in 2006 the federal estate-tax exemption jumped from $1.5 million to $2 million. Today there is no estate tax—but I'm betting new legislation will eventually change that. When tax laws change, your estate plan may need to change, too.
- **Nontax laws change** State legislatures exist to make laws; that's what they do. So they frequently change laws. Some changes could affect who receives your assets or how your trust is allowed to be managed. Lawyers stay on top of the latest changes and can help you determine what adjustments you should make to your estate plan to deal with any changes in nontax law.
- **You receive an inheritance** If you or your spouse received or think you will soon receive a significant inheritance, the increased value of your estate may cause you to change how your assets will be distributed upon your death.
- **You acquire or sell major assets** Say you purchase a business. If you do, you'll need a succession plan to ensure that the business stays in the hands of those you choose. If you sell a business, the proceeds may increase your wealth to the degree that you want to change your estate plan. Or, if you've gotten married or had children, new beneficiary designations for life insurance or IRAs must be carefully coordinated with the estate plan.
- **You move to another state** Estate planning documents are typically valid between jurisdictions, but every state has its own regulations and requirements. For example, a couple that moves from what is considered a "separate property state" like Virginia to a "community property state" like California might want to convert separate property to community property to

take advantage of certain income tax provisions. Plus, simply moving from state to state may also change how much state tax you pay on income. Some states tax income at a relatively high rate while other states have low or even nonexistent income taxes. Moving may result in adapting your estate plan to take advantage—or reduce the damage—of different state laws and guidelines.

Keep in mind that it's likely you won't realize when your estate plan should be changed, unless you are a lawyer. That's why having a periodic review with your lawyer is so important; your lawyer can ask a few questions, determine what changes need to be made . . . and keep you up-to-date.

Pay Attention to Beneficiaries

One last thing before we leave the topic of estate planning. No matter how hard you work to set up a great estate plan that protects your family and carries out your wishes . . . you can still go astray if you don't pay attention.

How? Beneficiary designations.

For example, say you took out a 20-year term life insurance policy a number of years ago. You were married at the time and named your wife as the beneficiary. You've paid the premium every year . . . but a few years ago you and your wife were divorced. You've since remarried and naturally want your estate to pass to your new wife.

But did you change your beneficiary designation on your "old" life insurance policy? If you didn't, and you pass away, the proceeds will go to the beneficiary of that policy—your ex-wife—even if you name your current wife in all your other estate-planning documents.

Beneficiary designations typically "trump" estate-planning documents. That holds true for financial accounts, like 401(k) plans and IRAs as well. When you review your estate plan, take the time to review the beneficiaries of any life insurance policies and financial accounts.

Keep those up-to-date and current as well.

Your Estate Plan: Gain Control

Even if it was set up recently, if major personal or financial events or changes have occurred (like marriage, the birth of a child, divorce, or selling or buying a business) review your estate plan with your attorney on a regular basis to make sure that your plan incorporates changes to your life and intentions.

If your personal situation hasn't changed, perform a periodic review to assess the impact of federal or state laws on the provisions of your trust.

Estate planning is a lifelong activity—make sure that the "back end" of the Way2Wealth is as well planned as the "front end."

- Set up a Revocable Living Trust and Pourover Will.
  Help your beneficiaries with the cost and delay of probate—and ensure that your wishes are carried out.
- Create a Health-Care Power of Attorney.
  It's your life and your health—if you are incapacitated, make sure that what you *want* to happen *is* what will happen.
- Create a HIPAA Power of Attorney.
  Make sure that someone can get the information they need to make decisions for you.
- Create a Property Power of Attorney.
  Don't let your affairs sit idle if you are unable to act for yourself.
- Establish a Family Retirement Preservation Trust.
  You worked hard to build tax-deferred wealth; make sure that your children can enjoy it on their terms, too.
- Write an Estate Planning Letter.
  Ensure that your grandfather's watch goes to your oldest son . . . or whoever *you* decide should have it.
- Review your plan on a regular basis.
  Plans and situations change—make sure that your estate plan reflects today's reality, not yesterday's.

While we're putting financial and legal safeguards in place, let's go one step farther and look at the insurance coverage you do—and probably don't—need.

CHAPTER 8

Position Before Submission
ANALYZE INSURANCE NEEDS

*Everything about a fight is unexpected. Every fight is different
and every fighter is different. But there is no reason to fear the
unexpected, especially if you are prepared. When you're unsure
about an opponent's skills, start with defense. Expect every fighter to
be the best fighter you have ever fought, because anyone can land a
punch. Expect and prepare to fight an Ali, a Machado, or a Gracie.
Expect the best and you will never be surprised.*

—Renzo Gracie

*Everyone buys insurance to protect their assets, but what is your
greatest asset? Is it your car? Your home? Your life? Sure, your life
is invaluable . . . but your greatest asset is your ability to generate
an income. Disability insurance protects you if you aren't able to
generate an income, and can be especially important if both spouses
generate an income. If something happens to one or both of you and
you can no longer work . . . how will you make a living?"*

—Alan Weiss

In Brazilian Jiu-Jitsu the phrase "position before submission" is
commonly used. What does it mean? Like most common principles,

"position before submission" carries different meanings at different levels of the sport. Like investing, simple principles can become complex; so can the idea of position before submission.

For beginners, position before submission is based on protection and security. Great teachers make sure that beginners focus on the basics. Instead of learning complicated submission holds, beginners learn to maintain fundamental positions like the guard, the mount, the cross body position, and the back mount. In those positions they establish balance and control . . . and then once the position is established they can seek a submission hold. Fighters who don't learn to establish and maintain the basic positions never advance particularly far—they lack the fundamentals necessary to protect themselves and establish a firm foundation for more complex moves.

Position for submission, in financial terms, is a lot like insurance. When I'm rolling, the principle of position before submission is the way I not only safeguard myself against the unexpected but it also helps me feel confident and relaxed. In my financial life, insurance helps reduce or eliminate some of my concerns or worries about unpredictable or unexpected events.

Protect Yourself—But Not to the Extreme

So if insurance is a good thing, a lot of insurance is a great thing, right?

Not necessarily. Think about insurance in Brazilian Jiu-Jitsu terms. If I focus solely on position—on protecting myself—I can to a large degree control a fight, but where will my offense come from? How will I move from position to submission if I spend all my time and energy worrying about my position? The same thing happens where insurance is concerned: Many people feel that the more insurance coverage they have the better off they will be . . . and that is simply not true.

Here's a quick example. Take auto insurance. The cost of auto insurance policies, like many other types of insurance, is based in part on the amount of deductible selected. A deductible is the amount you pay to repair the vehicle after an accident. For example, if you have a $250 deductible on collision claims—meaning repairs required due to an accident—you pay the first $250 of that expense. If the total repair cost comes to $1,000, you pay the first $250, and your insurance company pays the remainder. The higher your deductible, the lower your premium because the insurance company faces less risk if an accident occurs. By selecting a higher deductible you shift more of the risk onto yourself and away from the insurance company. Like most things in life, it's a give and take premise.

So, say you can take out an insurance policy with a $250 deductible or a $500 deductible. Selecting a $250 deductible certainly exposes you to less risk, because you will only have to pay $250 if you are in an accident, but at the same time costs you $130 more every six months. (Again, the insurance company charges more because it, not you, faces more risk.) If you are not involved in an accident in the next two years, the higher premium cost you $260, which is more than the amount it would have saved you if you had to file a claim. And every following year you go deeper into the hole. If you're like most people and only need to file a claim every five to eight years . . . you lost money by worrying more about position than submission.

Let's look at the different types of insurance available. I focus on the basics:

- Life insurance
- Auto insurance
- Property insurance
- Health insurance
- Disability insurance

Again, although I feel that many people are overinsured, at the same time insurance is a key element in any financial plan. As you journey along the Way2Wealth, you'll naturally run into road blocks and pitfalls; insurance can protect you from financial disaster and provide long-term security for your family.

Life Insurance

Many people call life insurance "death insurance," because the policy only pays off if you pass away. The goal of life insurance is to provide for the people you leave behind and can no longer support.

I know this will sound simple, but life insurance is designed to offset the loss of income your family will face and provide for their immediate needs. Life insurance is like a safety net—it's not an odd form of lottery ticket.

Yet many people view life insurance as just that: A way to ensure that their families are "wealthy" if they pass away. As a result they purchase policies that are far in excess of what is needed or even sensible. Think about it: Regardless of how it may seem when you watch the news, if you live in this country your odds of dying unexpectedly are low. Most people live long, full lives. The average person who is 30 years old today is expected to live to be around 80; if that is the case for you, what are the odds that you need to provide your family with millions of dollars in life insurance coverage?

And if you don't have kids and aren't married . . . do you need life insurance at all?

Before we look at the basic types of life insurance, let's determine how much coverage you really need.

Life Insurance: What Coverage Do You Need?

As I mentioned, life insurance is designed to replace your income if you pass away. So start there: What is your annual income? For the sake of this exercise, we'll assume you make $40,000 a year.

Now immediately bump that number down. You pay tax on your income; I assume those taxes add up to about 30 percent of your gross pay, meaning that you bring home approximately $26,000 per year. (Don't you love taxes? That's why I look at ways to ease your tax burden Chapter 8.) If you pass away, your family doesn't lose $40,000 a year in income; effectively it loses $26,000 in spendable income. (Keep in mind that I'm intentionally keeping things simple; a good insurance agent can help you determine exactly what will happen under different income and income tax scenarios.)

Why do I care about the effect of taxes? Generally speaking, your beneficiaries will not have to pay tax on a life insurance death benefit. (If the policy includes some type of investment component, your heirs may be required to pay taxes on the additional amount the policy has earned.) To keep things simple, I'll assume that your heirs will not owe any taxes on the money they receive—that's why replacing your net income is important, not replacing your gross income.

So, in order for your family to receive the same amount of income, you need to "replace" $26,000 per year. Of course you probably would have earned more in the future, especially if you are relatively young. At the same time, your family's expenses will likely decrease in the future because your kids will grow up and eventually leave the nest, and your wife may get a job, enjoy a bigger income . . . who knows what the future will hold. So again, to keep things simple, I'll just assume you need to replace $26,000 per year.

So say you're 30 years old. If you planned to work until you were 67, that's 37 years of income. Multiply 37 by $26,000 and your family needs $962,000 in coverage—basically $1 million in coverage. Keep in mind that under our worst-case scenario that's a conservative number; if your spouse takes a lump-sum payout, she can invest the majority of that money and make it go much farther over the years. For example, if she invests $500,000 of the proceeds and receives a 5 percent average return for 20 years, before taxes the original $500,000 will be worth more than $1.3 million.

So under this scenario, do you need more than $1 million in life insurance coverage? In my opinion, the answer is no. But there are other factors to take into account. You may want to provide for your children's education. You may have other situations you want to cover. Just keep in mind that using life insurance to create a "dream scenario" for your family is probably unrealistic—and expensive. Get coverage that your family needs, not that your family may "want."

Every situation is different. Every family's needs are different. Talk to an insurance agent about your current income, your expected income, and your family's future needs. Focus on determining the amount of coverage that will provide for your family but that is also affordable and fits within your overall wealth plan. Life insurance is an investment that only pays off if you die; other investments can pay off under almost any circumstances. Chances are you and your family will one day take advantage of the proceeds of your other investments, not your life insurance "investment."

Then, once you determine how much coverage you need, it's time to determine the type of insurance to purchase.

Types of Life Insurance

Life insurance comes in two basic flavors, and with two different intents. Life insurance is designed to provide protection, but some policies are also designed to act as investments as well. Term insurance provides protection; cash value policies provide protection and are investments as well. Let's take a closer look at both types of insurance.

Term Insurance   Term insurance is a "protection only" form of life insurance. A term insurance policy only pays a benefit if, you guessed it, you pass away. (In that way term life insurance is much like an auto insurance policy, because auto policies only pay off if you file a claim.) Because a term policy only pays when the insured party dies, premiums are relatively cheaper than whole life premiums.

Term policies come in a variety of flavors, but there are three basic types:

1. **Level Term**   The premiums and the death benefit stay level for a specific period of time. For example, say you purchase a $1 million, 20-year term life insurance policy. You pay a fixed premium each year, and if you die within that time period the policy pays your beneficiary $1 million. When the 20-year period expires, so does your coverage. At that point you can opt to take out a new policy.

2. **Renewable Term**   The death benefit stays level, but your premiums increase on an annual basis because the likelihood of your passing away increases every year. So

if you have a 20-year, $1 million policy, your premiums may start at something around $500 per year but could increase every year. Renewable term policies tend to have a "cap" amount, or a premium that cannot be exceeded. For example, your "cap" could be $800 per year, meaning that the insurance company cannot raise annual premiums over that amount during the term of the policy.

3. **Decreasing Term**   The premiums stay level but the death benefit reduces over the term of the policy. The principle behind a decreasing term policy is that the likelihood of your dying increases over the years, so to offset that risk the insurance company will pay off a lower amount to your beneficiaries. A common form of decreasing term life insurance is a mortgage insurance policy. If you have a mortgage insurance policy, as you pay down the balance of your mortgage your insurance coverage automatically goes down because the amount the insurance company will have to pay off if you die gets lower and lower every year (but your premiums typically stay the same).

Which type of term insurance makes sense for you? Hold on to that thought; you'll revisit it in a moment. For now let's look at the other type of life insurance policy:

Cash Value   Cash value policies are often called whole life policies, but as you'll see that's a somewhat inaccurate way to describe a cash value policy. Cash value policies provide a death benefit and have an investment component as well. If you pass away, your beneficiaries receive a death benefit; if you don't, you can under certain conditions "cash out" the policy and collect the current value of the policy. (With a term policy there is no cash value created—unless you die, of course.)

Cash value policies come in four basic types:

1. **Whole life**   Whole life policies are what most people think of when they think of cash value policies. Whole life

policies provide a guaranteed death benefit, require level premiums, and often result in a cash value separate from the death benefit value of the policy. You pay premiums, and a cash value is created based on investments made by the insurance company with those premiums. It takes a while for a cash value policy to build up a significant cash value, because the investments tend to grow at a relatively slow rate. If you like, think of a whole life policy as a term policy with limited investment benefits, too.

2. **Universal life**   Universal life policies are like whole life policies, but with added flexibility. Typically your premium is based on two factors: A portion of the premium covers the premium to provide a term insurance policy that will pay a defined death benefit, and a portion of your premium is deposited into an investment vehicle that earns interest and eventually creates a cash value. Universal policies are somewhat flexible because you can elect to pay higher premiums—therefore putting more money into the investment fund—or lower premiums—as long as your premium covers the term portion of the payment. In some cases you can even skip a premium payment or two as long as your investment "fund" is big enough to cover the cost of the premiums you skip.

3. **Variable life**   Variable life is like a universal life, but in this case you get to make decisions about how the cash value portion of your policy is invested. Different types of investments generate different levels of return, so the cash value of your policy varies depending on how your investments perform.

4. **Variable universal life**   (Yes, it's getting complicated.) Variable universal life is a combination of a universal life policy and a variable life policy. You can choose investments but also can choose to make lower or higher premium payments.

Confused? That's okay. Now that you understand the basics, let's take a step back.

Why are you buying life insurance in the first place? Do you only want to provide for your family? Do you want to provide for your family and create an investment vehicle at the same time?

If you are only worried about providing for your family, choose a term life insurance policy. Premiums tend to be significantly lower so you will more easily be able to afford coverage with a relatively high death benefit.

If the thought of enjoying an investment component within the policy is appealing, talk to your agent about the different types of cash value policies. The agent can explain the ins and outs of each type of policy and can help you determine which makes sense for your individual needs and situation.

But before you take out the policy, review your options with your wealth advisor. You may be able to generate a better return through other investment vehicles, like mutual funds or annuities. For example, you might decide to take a term policy and invest the additional money you would have paid in cash value premiums into a separate investment that can generate better returns over the long term. Just because a cash value policy has some amount of cash value doesn't mean it's a great investment. All insurance policies—like all investments—are not created equally.

Life Insurance Action Steps

1. Determine the amount of coverage you need.
2. Check out what your employer offers. Most employers offer term life insurance as an employee benefit, and the rates tend to be significantly cheaper than when you take out a policy on your own.
3. Shop around and find the best combination of terms, rates, and coverage for your needs.
4. Talk to your wealth advisor to see if cash value policies make sense for your investment goals.

Quick note: Many employers offer life insurance coverage for the children of employees. Usually the death benefit is relatively low, ranging from $5,000 per child up to around $30,000. Before you take out a policy with a high death benefit, take a moment and think about the purpose of life insurance. Life insurance is designed to replace income; do your children generate an income? Probably not . . . so what will you replace if they die (in financial terms)? Buying life insurance on your children makes sense if you want to ensure that you will have sufficient funds available to cover the cost of a funeral; buying life insurance to cover their lost income does not. Take the difference in premiums and invest it somewhere else.

Prepare for the Physical

Life insurance policies typically require a physical unless the policy is part of your employee benefits plan at work. Insurance companies check your heart rate, blood pressure, and typically draw blood for additional tests. Many check blood sugar scores, a test designed to help predict the risk of diabetes, and check cholesterol levels, a test designed to help predict the risk of heart disease.

The results of your physical will play a role in the amount of premium you are required to pay; if you are considered to be in poor health, your premiums will be higher because you are considered a greater risk.

So keep in mind that when a nurse or health-care provider takes your blood sample to run these tests the results could be affected based on what you did and ate the day before.

Why? Blood sugar levels can vary by 30 percent to 50 percent depending on recent meals; that's a result that could increase your premiums dramatically. Avoid high cholesterol and high salt foods for 24 hours before the physical. Don't eat a lot of sugar or take in caffeine—focus on drinking water for at least 8 to 10 hours before the physical.

And don't engage in strenuous activity for about 24 hours ahead of time—that will help keep your blood pressure down. Your goal isn't to "game" the insurance system; your goal is to make sure you don't inadvertently create a test result that costs you hundreds or thousands of dollars in the long run.

Auto Insurance

I feel sure that if you have a car you understand the basics of auto insurance. So instead of discussing how policies work, let's focus on ways you can reduce the cost of auto insurance while still protecting yourself from loss.

Step 1: Review Your Deductibles

The quickest way to cut auto insurance premiums is to increase your deductible to at least $500—if it's not already at that level. The savings generated by increasing your deductible could end up between 10 and 30 percent every six months. If you're a safe driver you might even consider raising your deductible to $1,000, especially if you have a decent amount of money in your emergency fund that can cover the cost of repairs. Weigh the risk, weigh the rewards, and select a deductible amount that is affordable and also provides decent coverage based on your situation and needs.

Step 2: Drop Towing Insurance

If your car breaks down, it might be comforting to know you will be reimbursed for the cost of towing, but be realistic: How often does your car need to be towed? Towing insurance premiums range from $15 to $30 every six months; put that money to work for you instead.

Step 3: Ask for Discounts

You might qualify for discounts based on a variety of scenarios:

- If you drive a low number of miles per year.
- If you have completed a driver safety course.
- If a student is away at college.
- If your child is a student who gets good grades.
- If your car has safety features like air bags and alarms.

Different insurance companies provide different types of discounts; the only way to know what you qualify for is to ask.

Step 4: Drop Coverage You No Longer Need

Most people don't pay cash for their vehicles. Lenders typically require borrowers to maintain collision and comprehensive coverage on their vehicles. That policy makes sense from the lender's point of view, because the car is the collateral used to secure the loan and the lender wants to make sure that collateral maintains a certain value, especially if it is involved in an accident.

But what if you have paid off your vehicle? Should you continue to carry comprehensive or collision coverage, or should you drop the coverage on that vehicle to liability-only?

The answer depends on several factors: How much the car is worth, how safely you drive, and how much money you have in your emergency fund. Dropping collision and comprehensive coverage is another form of risk-reward analysis: The risk is that the car will be damaged and you will have to pay for repairs out of your pocket. The reward occurs if the car is not damaged and you keep the additional premiums in your pocket.

A major factor to consider is the value of the car—not what it is worth to you, but what the insurance company feels it is worth. Auto insurance policies reimburse you for the value of the car, not what it costs to replace the car. If your car is fairly old and is only worth, say, $2,000, then paying hundreds of dollars every six months for collision and comprehensive coverage—with a deductible of $500 or $1,000—probably doesn't make good economic sense. On the other hand, if your car is still worth $30,000, carrying collision and comprehensive coverage probably makes great sense, because if the car is totaled you face a serious loss.

So although I can't tell you exactly what to do based on your situation, I can tell you not to forget to frequently review your policy and decide if you still need the same amount of coverage. Situations and needs change; don't be lazy and continue to pay premiums you no longer need to pay.

Step 5: Hold Off on Buying a New Car

Granted this isn't really an "insurance reduction" step, but it can certainly be considered a way to save on car insurance (and many other expenses). Most cars last 8 to 10 years before service costs start to add up. If you keep your current vehicle in good shape and pay if off, not only will you save on monthly payments but your insurance costs will also go down as the value of your car goes down. That's one case where you don't mind when an asset loses value. Insuring a new car is relatively expensive; when you decide to go car shopping, just keep in mind that the total cost is more than just the price of the car.

Again, auto insurance is a necessity—make sure that you get the coverage you need . . . but no more. Take advantage of discounts, be smart about deductibles, and shop around. If you don't already, talk to the agent who provides your homeowners insurance; typically you can save money on both policies if you purchase them from the same insurance company.

Property Insurance

For most people property insurance means homeowner's insurance. Aside from your vehicles, your home is likely to be the only other property you need to insure. That is unless you own a business, in which case you'll need a variety of business insurance coverage.

Homeowner's insurance is another basic type of insurance. Shop around for a policy that meets your needs and offers the best value . . . and keep one basic concept in mind:

Cash value is very different from replacement value.

Cash value is what the insurance company feels is the actual value of an item. For example, say you buy a sofa, so it's covered under your homeowner's policy. You paid $2,000 for it. Five years from now, although the sofa might cost you $2,000 (or more) to replace, it will only be worth a fraction of that amount, because the insurance company rightly assumes it will have depreciated due to normal wear and tear. So if, say, your home and the sofa is damaged by a fire, although it might cost you $2,000 or more to replace that sofa . . . you may only receive $500 or less from the insurance company.

The same holds true for your home. If you insure a home you purchase for $200,000, you're covered—at least for now. But if property values increase, your policy coverage may not increase to reflect new values. If the home burns to the ground 10 years from now, and your policy was not adjusted . . . you may only receive a fraction of the amount required to rebuild it (and replace furnishings and other possessions).

Replacement value is the amount required to replace an item. Replacement value policies do just what they say: They replace the items that are damaged or lost, minus any deductible.

Keep in mind that some policies do put a cap on replacement value. For example, a policy may specify that it will pay replacement value up to a certain percentage of cash value. If your policy caps replacement value at 200 percent of cash value, and your sofa was worth $500, the policy will only pay $1,000, even though replacing the couch might cost $2,000 or more.

Now: Guess which type of policy is better for you?

Replacement value policies, obviously. Many homeowners policies provide coverage based on replacement value, but don't assume. Make sure you know.

You can also add additional coverage to your policy, like:

- Guaranteed replacement cost, designed to pay the full cost of rebuilding your home.
- Extended replacement cost, which insures your home for a certain value and adds a 20 to 25 percent "extended limit" if construction costs go higher than expected.
- Inflation protection, which increases the amount of coverage so that it keeps pace with normal inflation rates.
- Property theft, which covers items outside the home, like personal items in your vehicle, a trailer, or a boat.
- "Riders" that cover personal possessions outside the limits of a normal policy. For example, say you own a number of antiques and keep them in your home; the average homeowner's policy will not cover expensive antiques. In that case a rider (basically a rider is an insurance term referring to extensions or additions to your policy) can cover those unusual or expensive items. You will pay an additional premium for that coverage. If you have expensive items, don't assume that your standard policy will cover them.

The key with homeowners insurance—and all property insurance—is to cover your risks, protect your assets . . . but to be sensible. Think position before submission . . . but don't insure yourself to the point that you spend so much in premiums you have no other investment options available. Insurance can help make sure you don't "lose," but insurance will never help you "win."

Health Insurance

Millions of Americans don't have health insurance, although the recent health-care bill is designed to change that fact, at least to a degree. Health insurance is a key part of any financial plan—especially major medical insurance.

If you are fortunate enough to be offered coverage by your employer, take it. Choosing not to be covered simply to save a little money makes little sense. You can cut your costs slightly by taking coverage with a higher deductible (if your employer's coverage gives you that option), but otherwise be happy that you and your family can receive affordable health-care coverage.

If you have to purchase an individual health-care policy you'll spend much more; although the cost varies, the average family of four is likely to have to spend between $800 and $1,200 per month on private health-care coverage. Choosing a higher deductible is one way to reduce the cost; also consider whether you need to carry coverage for things like eye care.

Also focus on the major medical portion of your insurance. Major medical covers serious, long-term care required for major illnesses or injuries. Major medical coverage tends to be less expensive than standard coverage, because most people go to the doctor for minor issues but relatively few are incapacitated or sick for long periods of time.

Disability Insurance

At the beginning of this chapter, my friend Alan Weiss made a great point: Most people think about insurance to protect themselves from property loss . . . but many people forget that their biggest asset is their ability to generate an income. Statistics vary, but it appears that less than one-third of Americans carry disability insurance.

But what happens if you can't work—for weeks, months, or even years?

Disability policies vary widely. Here are the basic elements of a disability policy:

Waiting Period   The waiting period is the number of days that must elapse before you are allowed to start receiving insurance payments. For example, if the waiting period is 60 days, you will not receive disability payments until 60 days after you suffered the illness or injury. In most cases payments are then retroactive to the date of illness or injury (but not always). Either way the waiting period is just that: The amount of time you have to wait until you start receiving payments. The shorter the waiting period, the better . . . but expect to pay more for shorter waiting periods.

Benefit Period   The benefit period is the amount of time you can receive disability payments. For example, if the benefit period is five years, you can receive payments for up to five years—but no longer. The longer the benefit period the better; the best case scenario is for the benefit period to last until you reach age 65 or more, when you would have retired.

Occupation   Benefits are determined based on your occupation; higher-rated occupations tend to have higher premiums but also longer benefit periods. Your occupation is also used to determine the risk of long-term injury; labor-intensive occupations expose people to greater risk. In some cases the occupation is used to determine the extent of benefits; if you are a surgeon and are injured and can no longer operate, you may still be able to work as a nonsurgical physician . . . meaning disability payments will be lower, because "replacing" your income is not completely necessary.

Benefit   The benefit amount (the amount of your disability payment) is typically a percentage of your current pay. Most disability policies do not provide more than 60 percent or so of the worker's pay, but disability benefits are typically tax-free, which offsets some of the difference. The higher the payout, the better . . . but you will pay more for higher percentage payouts.

Important note Premiums are based on a variety of factors, including your age. Get a disability policy when you are young and healthy; once you lock in your premium rate, it will not change. And if you lock in your policy at a specific benefit amount, if your income goes down you can still be covered at the higher rate. Don't wait—protect your income and pay less in the process. Check out the coverage offered by your employer, or if that is not available (or is not sufficient) talk to an independent insurance agent. Your current insurance agent is likely to offer disability coverage along with the other insurance he or she can provide.

Analyze Insurance Needs: Position before Submission

Insurance provides protection from loss. But insurance—except in certain situations—is not an investment. Get the coverage you need in order to protect your family.

- Get the right life insurance.
  Determine how much you need and what type of policy is right for you.
- Get the right auto insurance.
  Insure your vehicles . . . and save money in the process.
- Get the right property insurance.
  Make sure you can replace items that are damaged or lost.
- Get the right health insurance.
  Health insurance is absolutely vital; protect yourself and your family from the costs of illness and injury.
- Get the right disability insurance.
  Your greatest asset is your ability to generate an income; protect that asset.

(Continued)

Insurance is a fundamental component of the Way2Wealth. Failing to have the right insurance is like failing to learn the basics of the guard position; in certain situations you might find yourself helpless and without any options or ways to protect yourself.

And because I've talked so much about protecting yourself, let's go on the offensive and talk about life in "retirement"! (You'll see why I put quotation marks after the word retirement in a moment.)

CHAPTER 9

Attitude

LIFE IN RETIREMENT

*Don't assume that simply because you have a "retirement plan"
that you've done enough. Spend time thinking about the lifestyle
they want to have; it's never too early to plan what you want to do
and where you want to live. Retirement isn't simply a way to no
longer work. Think about your dreams. Set goals. If you don't have
goals you can't have a plan . . . and you travel a road that leads
nowhere. Retirement is a lot more than financial planning—what
do you want to do with your life?*

—Alan Weiss

*Planning for retirement—whatever that word means to you—boils
down to cash flow planning. If you don't have a handle on your
expenses and really track your expense correctly, both now and in
retirement, it will be a constant challenge to make sure you are
living within your means. It's hard work if you haven't done it.
But you have to. Sadly, people with millions of dollars don't sit
down and plan for their expenses, and most people underestimate
what they will need. And they don't anticipate change: Tax laws
may change, health care costs could increase, your relatives might
need help . . . so you really have to do the dirty work and think
ahead—or have someone help you do the dirty work.*

—Ron Carson

Let's get two things out of the way immediately:

One, this is probably the shortest chapter on "retirement planning" that you will ever read. Why?

Because two, I think that quite frankly the idea of retirement is a crock.

I never plan to retire. If retirement means sitting in a chair, watching TV, and watching the grass grow . . . I will never retire.

You shouldn't either. Why should your goal be to suddenly stop: Stop working, stop dreaming, stop achieving . . . stop *living* your life to the fullest?

So I don't think in terms of "retirement." I think of life as a series of stages. My goal is to someday build up sufficient assets so that I can make different choices about how I live my life. I want to support my church, provide for my family, help my children get started on their own paths . . . and at some point shift my focus into other areas.

I love working with clients and helping them try to reach their financial goals, and I will probably always do so, even if on a more limited basis.

But then I look forward to doing more for my church and my community.

I want to be more involved in teaching; I love interacting with people.

I want to enjoy spending more time learning Brazilian Jiu-Jitsu; I never plan to stop participating in the sport.

My wife and I want to travel more; and even though we love where we live, we may decide to move.

The point is that my wife and I are hard at work developing plans for the next stages of our lives; the details of those plans are not important to you—they are only important to us. What *is* important to you is your plans.

What do you want to do more of?

Where do you want to live?

How do you want to live?

And how much money will you need?

How Much Money Will You Need?

Where "retirement" is concerned, this is the first question everyone asks. The answer depends on your individual situation. Think back to what True Wealth means to you. What goals did you establish? What targets did you set? You are already a long way toward determining your path . . . just keep in mind that your goals may change over time—and that's okay!

Life is all about changing and adapting and growing—instead of fearing change, you should be glad that your plans do change because that means you're *living* your life and growing as a person.

Deciding how much you'll need when you "retire" is a fairly complicated process. A skilled wealth advisor knows what questions to ask and what variables to consider. Ask your wealth advisor to help you build your own scenarios based on what True Wealth means to you.

But to get you started, I can boil the process down to some simple steps and some simple equations. How much money you need is based on how much you will earn—from investments, from pensions and retirement funds, from Social Security (if it's still solvent), and from any jobs you have. Don't think you can't work when you are in your seventies; until recently the father of one of my friends drove a parts truck for an automotive dealership three days a week—and he was 77 years old! He didn't do it for the money. He loved getting out, interacting with people, and feeling useful and needed.

So let's take a couple of basic approaches to estimating what you will need when you "retire."

Current Spending Estimate

One way to decide how much you'll need is to base your calculations on what you currently spend. Start by answering some basic questions:

- **What is your definition of True Wealth?** What do you plan for the next stage in your life? Do you plan to live as you do currently in terms of expenses?

Many people assume they will spend as much or more than they currently spend, and that's okay. Others plan to live based on a lower standard of living: Smaller home, fewer cars . . . in order to "retire" earlier or set out on the next stage of their life even earlier.

There is no right or wrong answer to these questions. The only right answers are your answers. But you do need to know what you want to do before you can decide how you will get there.

- **What do you currently make?** Although the odds are what you currently earn will not be sufficient to support you in your next stage of life—unless you change careers—what you currently "live on" is a good starting point.
- **How much do you expect to receive from Social Security? Will you receive a pension when you retire?** Fewer and fewer companies are continuing to offer pensions to their employees, but it is possible that you have a plan in place with a previous employer. Most employers that offer pensions provide an annual projection of what you can expect in terms of pension benefits, based on how much you will earn and how long you will remain an employer of the company or organization.

   You can estimate your Social Security benefits by checking the statement you receive every year from the Social Security Administration.

- **When do you plan to "retire"?** The younger you are when you retire, the longer you should expect to live during your retirement. Clearly that is an obvious point, but it is also one many people fail to consider. The longer you will be retired, the more money you will need—meaning you'll need more in savings and investments. The longer you wait to retire the less you will need to draw from your savings, and the longer you will have to generate additional savings . . . but ultimately "when" is based on your definition of True Wealth.
- **What is your Family Benchmark?** And how do you plan to invest? Aggressive investments tend to carry higher returns

but greater risk; safer investments carry less risk but typically provide lower returns. "How much" is based on not only the amount you save but also the amount you earn on those savings, so how you plan to invest is a critical component in your plan.

- **What do you currently have?** The older you are and the less you currently have in retirement savings, the more you'll need to save in the future to hit your True Wealth target. If you have already managed to save a significant sum, you are off to a fine start. If you have no savings, the road ahead is a little tougher, and you'll need to put the Way2Wealth into immediate action.

Answering these questions is a great start. Using the answers I can do some simple math and determine how much you'll need.

For example, say you currently earn $40,000 per year, plan to retire when you are 65, and feel you will be more than happy to live on $40,000 when you retire. The average person can expect to live until he or she is approximately 80 years old, so I'll assume you will live for 25 more years.

So, for example, if you want to live on $40,000 per year, multiply $40,000 by 25. You'll need at least $1,000,000 in savings to live at that level of True Wealth.

But, if you expect to receive $15,000 in Social Security benefits, you will only need $25,000 of your own money to add up to $40,000 . . . meaning you will "only" need savings of $625,000.

And, if you will receive a pension of $6,000 per year, then the amount of money you will need to draw from savings goes down to $19,000 per year, for a total savings requirement of $475,000.

Obviously the real calculations and considerations are much more complicated; I didn't take into account taxes, inflation, changes in health care costs . . . the point is to give you a simple way to start thinking about retirement planning.

Here's another popular way to calculate how much you need when you retire. It's called the 10-10-4 Rule.

10-10-4 Rule

This approach is a little different. The 10-10-4 rule is based on the premise that:

- The average person will need to have approximately 10 times their current income in a retirement account.
- To save 10 times his or her income, the average person is likely to need to save 10 percent of his or her current income.
- And when a person retires, he or she should withdraw 4 percent of their retirement fund to use for living expenses.

How does this approach work in practice? To keep things simple, let's do a little basic math. Either of the "10"s in the equation can be used to calculate what you will need. For example, let's imagine that you are currently 30 years old and make $50,000 a year. Your goal is to retire when you are 65.

If you save 10 percent of your pay—perhaps in a 401(k) or IRA—and your pay stays flat throughout your career, then when you reach age 65 you will have more than $717,000 in your account if you average a 7 percent annual return. That's almost 20 times your annual pay, so from that point of view you're in good shape according to 10-10-4 rule. Then, if you withdraw 4 percent of the balance, you'll have a little less than $30,000 to spend each year.

Of course, if your employer matches 50 percent of your contribution, your 401(k) will be worth more than $1 million, meaning you can draw over $40,000 a year to spend. (That's why taking advantage of the employer match is so important.)

For fun, let's take a different approach. In this case I will assume you are 45 years old. If you save 10 percent of your pay each year, don't get an employer match, and earn 7 percent, you will only have about $210,000 in your account. (Save early, save often—take advantage of the power of compounding.) Since $210,000 is just over 4 times your current pay, the 10-10-4 rule doesn't work. You'll need to take a different approach.

In that case, use the other "10," the "10 times your current pay" 10. You currently make $50,000, and 10 times $50,000 is $500,000. You only have 20 years left to accumulate that sum, so you will need to save a little more than 23 percent of your pay, or about $12,000 per year each to reach your target.

Start soon.

These are just two basic approaches to determining what you will need. Neither is particularly scientific. Neither is in any way sufficient to develop a real plan you can put into effect.

Instead, my goal is to help you get a quick sense of what you will need. A wealth advisor can walk you step by step through a much more thorough process that will result in a much more concrete plan.

But again, the process starts with your definition of True Wealth and your Family Benchmark. What do you want to do? How do you want to live? What legacy do you want to leave behind?

How will you continue to live with purpose by thinking and acting with the end in mind?

That's True Wealth. That's real "retirement" planning.

Talk to your wealth advisor. He or she can help you try to achieve your vision of True Wealth. Retirement isn't an end result; "retirement" is simply a stage on the Way2Wealth.

Life in Retirement: Attitude

Please don't think of retirement as an end goal and the culmination of your life's work. "Retirement" is simply another phase in a well-lived life. Plan to make the transition from one stage on the Way2Wealth to another, as you are able to incorporate more and more of your vision of True Wealth into your daily life and the life of your family.

I will never retire—I hope you won't, either.

- Revisit your definition of True Wealth.
  What do you want to do? How do you want to live?
- Revisit your Family Benchmark.
  How will you get there?

(Continued)

- Do some quick math to determine where you stand.
  Apply a handy rule of thumb to determine how much you'll
    need to save, but then . . . .
- Talk to a wealth advisor and create a comprehensive plan.
  Without goals you can't create a plan . . . and without a plan
    you can't reach your goals.

"Retirement" planning never ends because your goals and dreams will constantly change. That's not a problem—that's great! Although you may not "work" in the strictest sense, if you live your life to the fullest you will always be "working" with a purpose and a goal in mind: Whether to change careers, to help others, to spend more time with your family, to give back . . . so create a plan and work hard to accomplish that plan.

Don't let the pain of regret hit you when you are ready to move on to a new stage in your life.

CHAPTER

Leverage

ESTABLISH YOUR TAX PLAN

Strength is a small part of the Brazilian Jiu-Jitsu equation. Watch great fighters and it appears they are expending very little energy or effort. Great Brazilian Jiu-Jitsu fighters don't work hard . . . they work smart. Leverage is the key to using force efficiently and making the most of your skills and your strength. Every black belt I know has what amounts to a Ph.D. in the principles of leverage.

—Luke Rinehart

I can't tell you how many times even the most sophisticated investors forget to think about tax planning. Many people don't focus on using a proactive tax plan to defer income, offset gains by taking losses, switching to tax-advantaged investments. . . . Tax planning is a key part of any investment plan. Not thinking about tax planning is like focusing on how much you make instead of how much you spend—it's not what you make that is important . . . it's what you keep.

—Alan Weiss

I love my friend Alan's quote: "It's not what you *make* that is important . . . it's what you *keep*."

After all, do you get to spend the amount of gross pay that appears on your paycheck? Of course not; what's left—your take-home pay—is what you get to pay.

That's why taking steps to legally decrease the amount of taxes you pay and increase the amount of money that goes in your pockets—and your investments—is so important. Think of your pay and your investments earnings as your strength; then apply tax planning, or leverage, to that pay and those investments so that they go even farther.

But before diving in, keep in mind that the subject of taxes and tax planning can be incredibly complicated. The rules change almost every year: Deductions that were available last year are no longer available, and other deductions and tax strategies have taken their place. Keeping up with tax laws is a full-time job.

So with that said, here's my best advice: Unless you are not married, have no kids, don't own your home, have no investments and no assets to speak of . . . get help from an accountant or skilled tax advisor. And don't wait until tax time rolls around; start planning ways to cut your taxes on this year's income now. If you wait until tax time, it's usually too late. In most cases a skilled tax advisor will save you much more than you pay in fees. Talk to your wealth advisor and get referrals and recommendations; the Way2Wealth is based on teamwork and great coaching, not on going it alone in a futile attempt to save a few dollars on fees.

Great advice is almost always worth more than you pay for it. Even a Brazilian Jiu-Jitsu superstar like Renzo Gracie takes advice and gets input from other martial artists.

He told me:

> There is no color, no religion, no class system, and no racism on the mats. On the mats a man or woman is as good as the knowledge they receive and the knowledge they share. The moment you exchange knowledge you grow. The moment you lock yourself in a box and don't try to learn from others and help others improve, you fade. My grandfather's biggest gift to me was

teaching me that everyone is basically the same: The only thing that sets us apart is how we think. If we accept someone else's wisdom, culture, thoughts, ideas . . . we are all better people and we help create a better world.

If a guy like Renzo thinks he can always learn from others, shouldn't you? That's why the following is designed to give you a sense of the possibilities involved in tax planning; see a skilled tax advisor for specific advice that can help you apply the power of leverage to your income and your investments.

Tax Savings: Homeowners

Owning a home creates a number of tax advantages.

Mortgage points   The IRS generally allows you to deduct points you pay when you take out a mortgage. Each point equals 1 percent of your loan; if you borrow $100,000, one point is $1,000. You pay points when you close on the house. Many people choose to pay points in order to get a lower interest rate on their mortgages. In some cases paying additional points might be a good idea, in other cases it could work to your disadvantage. Work through all the scenarios before you decide to pay or not to pay points.

You can spread your deduction for mortgage points over the term of the loan or deduct them fully for the year they were paid. To qualify to fully deduct points, in one year, the house you buy must be used as your main residence—it can't be an investment property.

Mortgage interest   In most cases you can deduct all the interest you pay on a home mortgage. That includes mortgages for a primary home, a second home or vacation property, and home equity loans, as long as the value of your home meets certain guidelines.

Mortgage insurance   You will almost always be required to purchase private mortgage insurance (PMI) if your down payment is less than 20 percent of the cost of the home. If you purchased a home from 2007 through this year, you should qualify to deduct all or at least a portion of the mortgage insurance premium you pay.

A few restrictions do apply to private mortgage insurance deductions, though. For example, your adjusted gross income can't be more than $109,000 ($54,500 if you're married but filing separately).

Tax Savings: Students and Their Parents

Many students—or more likely you, the parents—qualify for tuition and fees deductions or student loan interest deductions.

American Opportunity Tax Credit   This is a new tax credit that is an element of the American Recovery and Reinvestment Act. The goal of this tax credit is in large part to replace the Hope Tax Credit. Qualifying taxpayers get a $2,500 credit per student enrolled in college. If you have two kids in college, you can claim $5,000 in tax credits. The credit is determined based on the following formula:

- A dollar-for-dollar credit on the first $2,000 of education costs.
- 25 percent of the remaining education costs up to a total of $2,500. If that sounds complicated, think of it this way: If you spend $4,000 or more on your child's education in a year, you qualify for the full $2,500 credit.

The American Opportunity Tax Credit starts to phase out for single taxpayers with modified adjusted gross incomes between $80,000 and $90,000; the phaseout starts between $160,000 and $180,000 for married couples who file jointly. If you exceed certain income limits you no longer qualify.

One neat fact is that the American Opportunity Tax Credit is what is considered a "top line" tax credit. You are not required to file itemized deductions in order to qualify for the credit.

Lifetime Learning Tax Credit The Lifetime Learning credit does not require a student to maintain a specific number of credit hours and is available for an unlimited number of years. And, unlike some other programs, graduate students can also qualify.

The Lifetime Learning Tax Credit is up to a maximum of $2,000 per year, based on a 20 percent annual credit on tuition and fees. So, if you spend $10,000 on college expenses you max out the credit you can receive. If you spend $4,000 the result is an $800 credit.

Expenses that qualify include tuition and fees for yourself, your spouse, and any other individual you claim as a dependent when you file your tax return.

But keep in mind that qualification rules are likely to change every year, and credits are phased out depending on the amount of your adjusted gross income.

Tuition and Fees Here's where it starts to get a little tricky. Instead of taking certain tax credits, you might decide use the tuition and fees deduction instead. If you do, you can deduct up to $4,000 of qualifying education costs. You won't qualify if your modified adjusted gross income is more than $65,000 (if you file as single) or $130,000 (if you file as married filing jointly).

Also keep in mind that any expenses that are paid from a qualifying Section 529 plan (which I talk about later) will not be considered as expenses that qualify.

Plus, the $4,000 maximum deduction is an annual maximum and is regardless of the number of students in your household. If you only have one child in college the tuition and fees deduction is probably your best bet. If you have two or more children in college at the same time, taking the American Opportunity Tax Credit is probably the better option.

Private College Grant Some states give grants to students who attend in-state private colleges instead of state-funded colleges and universities. Take the state of Virginia, which provides a $2,500 grant per year for students who attend a private college. The goal of these grants is to support and promote enrollment at private colleges. Although I admit that a private college grant is not a tax credit, it does reduce the amount of money you will have to pay for your child's education, and it is provided by the government . . . so I'll call it a "tax credit."

Student Loan Interest Student loan interest can qualify for a tax deduction as long as the student actually used the loan funds for qualifying expenses like tuition, fees, room and board, and other education-related expenses. Qualifying taxpayers may be able to deduct up to $2,500 in interest per year. The government will let you know if you qualify. Anyone who paid $600 or more in interest receives a Form 1098-E Student Loan Interest Statement.

As a bonus, you are not required to itemize deductions to claim the student loan interest deduction.

College Saving Plans

State-sponsored college savings plans are a great deal for taxpayers because withdrawals made to pay college expenses for the plan's beneficiary (in other words, the student) are tax-free. The sooner you contribute to a plan, the less money you will need for college expenses.

Here are the basic types of college savings plans:

Prepaid tuition plans Prepaid tuition plans allow you to lock in a predetermined price for future college tuition costs. But these plans do come with restrictions. Prepaid plans include residency requirements, age restrictions, and limited enrollment periods. Prepaid plans also may not let you put aside money for room and board expenses or books, because most only cover tuition and required fees.

On the positive side, college tuition rates have tended to rise faster than the inflation rate, which might make a prepaid plan a good option as long as you intend to enroll your children in a public university in your state. You can make a one-time lump payment, or pay a monthly amount over a specified number of years. This setup is a little like paying off a loan, although in effect you pay off the loan before you receive the tuition.

529 savings plans   529 Plans tend to be more flexible than prepaid tuition plans. In most cases you're allowed to go to a school in any state. Plus, you may be allowed to choose how your money is invested, using mutual funds, money market funds, or bond funds. 529 Plan funds can be used to pay for "qualified" educational expenses like room and board, additional fees, books, computers . . . anything directly related to the student's education.

There are potential negatives, though. Unlike a prepaid tuition plan the money you put in a 529 Plan is subject to ups and downs in the investment market. A return is not guaranteed. Plus, you can't lock in costs now and pay the amount you lock in regardless of any college cost increases.

529 Plan contributions are not deductible from federal income taxes, but some contributions are often deductible at the state level, depending on specific conditions.

Contribution limits are pretty high: Most college savings plans allow a lump-sum contribution of more than $250,000. In many cases that much won't be necessary, especially if you plan for your child to attend a state (public) school instead of a private college. If you want to stay within gift-tax guidelines, you can spread contributions to the 520 Plan over a five-year period so that each contribution is less than $13,000 per year, which is the current gift tax. Under a 529 Plan you can claim five years of gift tax exclusions at one time, so if you are married you can contribute $26,000 per year, because you and your wife are each allowed to make a $13,000 contribution, for a total of five years, and avoid gift tax issues.

Some 529 Plans are state-specific while others let a student attend any institution in the country that qualifies.

In short, make sure you know exactly what you will receive for your money—both in terms of education and in terms of tax benefits.

Tax Savings: Retirement

I've covered the tax benefits of retirement savings plans already; here's a brief recap.

401(k)   401(k) plans are tax-deferred savings plans. You can deduct contributions from your current income tax, and your account will grow tax-free. You only pay taxes when you start to withdraw funds. Say you currently earn $30,000 and you contribute $1,000 of your pay to a 401(k) plan; at tax time your gross income is reduced to $29,000, not $30,000, and you only pay tax on that amount. And if your employer matches your contributions, you receive that money on a tax-deferred basis well.

Traditional IRA   Depending on your income you may be able to take a tax deduction for some or all of the contributions you make to a traditional IRA. Taxes are deferred; you pay tax on your contributions and earnings only when you begin withdrawing money from your account.

In short, you don't pay tax up front—you pay on the back end.

Although the requirements may change, you can currently contribute $5,000 to a traditional IRA, or $6,000 if you're 50 and older and are making what the IRS calls "catch up" contributions so you can put away a little more toward retirement.

Roth IRA   Unlike a traditional IRA you are not allowed to deduct from your income taxes contributions made to a Roth IRA. But there's a great tradeoff: The main benefit of a Roth IRA is that your earnings are withdrawn tax-free when you retire.

The current contribution limits are the same as apply for traditional IRAs.

These are the basics of tax planning. Want to know more? Talk to a tax advisor and get specific advice for your situation.

Why not do everything possible to legally limit the amount you pay in taxes?

Like Alan says, it's not what you make that is important . . . it's what you keep.

Establish Your Tax Plan: Leverage

Although "death and taxes" may be certain, how much tax you are required to pay is anything but certain. A tax advisor can help you create a plan that leverages your income and your earnings and creates another stepping stone on the Way2Wealth. Plan ahead; the pain of discipline where tax planning is concerned will greatly outweigh the pain of regret if you have failed to take advantage of the legal opportunities at your disposal.

- Get help.
  In most cases a tax advisor will save you much more than he or she charges.
- Take advantage of common deductions.
  Take deductions for owning a home, college expenses, retirement plans.
- If you haven't already, get help.

  Please don't go it alone; everyone needs a coach.

Tax planning is a lifelong task; at every stage of your life you can take advantage of different opportunities. That's why tax planning is one of the last—but one of the most important—steps along the Way2Wealth. Whether you're just joining the workforce or have been retired for years, tax planning can and will pay off.

What's left? Time to hit the showers: Time to rinse and repeat!

Love, Discipline, and Dedication

HAVE YOUR PLAN UPDATED

Working towards your goals is not a "sometimes" thing. You have to continue to grow and progress and practice, otherwise you'll go backwards. Stick to your plan, stay disciplined, and build for the long run. I started in Brazilian Jiu-Jitsu for confidence and self-esteem. Now I do it for sport, for excitement, and for achievement. Work hard on the things you love and good things will happen.

—Jim Lake

I am a shark, the ground is my ocean . . . and most people can't even swim.

—Rickson Gracie

You've come a long way, but you are in no way done. The Way2Wealth is a lifelong journey. The best plans constantly evolve and change based on changes in your personal life and the world around you. For example, say:

- Your definition of True Wealth changes.
- Your short- or long-term goals change.
- You change careers.
- You get married, divorced, have kids.

- You face a serious illness or injury.
- The economy dips—or explodes.
- Investment earnings change radically.
- Tax laws change.

As a result, even the best plans will need to adapt and evolve. Yours should, too.

What should you do?

First, constantly remind yourself of nine basic principles of financial success:

1. Give back.
2. Pay yourself first.
3. Automate the process—make saving and investing automatic.
4. Maintain a cash safety net—build an emergency savings fund.
5. Manage credit wisely—borrow when it's to your advantage.
6. Get time on your side—invest early and often.
7. Never procrastinate.
8. Make reality your perception—get the facts, be informed, and expand your knowledge.
9. Follow a simple and comprehensive strategy.

Each of these principles is important, but the last point is especially critical. Building wealth and achieving financial freedom is not incredibly complicated. Building wealth is based on using strategies that minimize risk, maximize return, and are focused on helping you pursue your individual goals.

That's why your plan will constantly change and evolve. Your goals will change, and so will the strategies you use to reach those goals.

Then, review your plan with your wealth advisor and tax advisor at least once a year—or more frequently. Stay in touch. Stay on top of your investments and your plans. Take an interest and feel a sense of ownership in your own future.

Don't just sit and listen; learn. Be involved in the process. People who commit themselves to putting in the time and effort are the ones most likely to succeed.

In short, it's your money and your future—take responsibility so you can do everything possible to ensure that you reach your goals.

The Way2Wealth can help you reach your goals . . . but you have to follow the path and make adjustments along the way. Don't just file your plans away and forget them—live your plans and you can live your dreams!

Conclusion

As I finish writing this book I'm reminded of a theory of success that is currently in vogue. A number of people feel that success is not simply based on talent. Sure, God gives us all talents and hopes we will use them . . . but successful people are successful because, quite frankly, they work harder than most other people.

For example, some experts feel that to master a skill takes years. The "magic number" often quoted is 10,000 hours; using this theory it takes 10,000 hours of concentrated, focused practice to truly master a complex skill. (For instance, like becoming a world-class musician, or an NFL quarterback . . . or a champion in Brazilian Jiu-Jitsu.)

The point? We are all born with certain qualities, but whether we succeed is based more on how hard we work than on our innate talents or abilities. The world is filled with talented people—the people who achieve great success outwork everyone else.

I believe in this theory, because in a way it encompasses how I have lived my life. I don't have advanced college degrees. I haven't taken esoteric financial courses. My list of credentials is nowhere near as long as some of my peers.

But I do have something extremely important on my side: I may not have the credentials . . . but I will outwork anyone. Put simply, you may be "smarter" than me . . . but I will outwork you any day of the week.

When I spoke with Sam Sheridan, the author of *A Fighter's Heart* and *The Fighter's Mind*, both great books, he had a fascinating point of view. He said:

> Marcelo Garcia is one of the top Brazilian Jiu-Jitsu fighters in the world. Why? He loves it more. He practices all day every day,

and it shows. He proves there are no "magic bullets." A common premise in Western thought and Western martial arts is that there is a "secret," and once you learn that secret, you're invincible. That is a fundamental misunderstanding: "Secrets" emerge after a lifetime of study. *Hard work* is the secret.

Along the same lines, a friend once told me that becoming a master of a martial art has nothing to do with mastering thousands of moves; becoming a master means performing a handful of moves thousands of times. He looks at it the way Sam does. There are no tricks.

There are no "special" moves.

The only trick is hard work.

That's why I love Brazilian Jiu-Jitsu. Brazilian Jiu-Jitsu is incredibly adaptable. Its techniques mold themselves to the individual. Dedication is the key; not talent or coordination or strength. Most martial arts rely on at least some basic level of athleticism, power, and flexibility; success in Jiu-Jitsu is based on dedication, knowledge, and effort.

So is following the Way2Wealth.

Working hard is how I succeed, in business and in life. I know what I want to achieve, and I try to let nothing stand in the way. That's how I developed the Way2Wealth. Over time I realized that simple principles, applied with discipline and diligence, lead to success. You don't need a finance degree. You don't need to spend hundreds of hours in classes. You don't need to read book after book after book. You simply need to apply basic principles, get sound advice, create your own vision of True Wealth . . . and work hard to achieve it.

If you do, you have every chance of success.

If you don't, you have no chance of success. Which would you rather bet on: winning the lottery, or relying on your own dedication and hard work to build the life for your family that you want them to live?

I'll take dedication and hard work any day.

Work the plan, and the plan can work for you.

SCOTT FORD

An Overview of the Development and Principles of Jiu-Jitsu

Although translated as "The Gentle Art," Jiu-Jitsu can be one of the most devastating martial arts ever created. The idea of the gentle art is not necessarily to be gentle with your opponent but to use minimum force to achieve maximum results. The main objective of Jiu-Jitsu is to close the distance between you and your opponents, throw or take them down to the ground, then control and submit them using a choke, arm lock, or leg lock. It is not an art built on athleticism and strength but on technique and leverage.

To be effective in Jiu-Jitsu one must understand the harmony of balance, timing, and leverage.

Balance is strength.

Imagine a smaller guy who can create a solid stance with his feet and a much bigger guy who stands in front of him with his feet tied together. When they go to push each other over, who do you think will win? Balance is strength and must always be established in Jiu-Jitsu. Although most techniques can be attempted at any time, timing is what truly gives them grace and purpose. Each technique has its time, and proper timing is what allows a technique to achieve its desired effect. Leverage gives one thing the ability to have more strength or effectiveness than another. In Jiu-Jitsu, leverage is based on understanding how to use your whole body to attack a portion of someone else's. In order to achieve maximum leverage in Jiu-Jitsu, one must understand proper body positioning as well as directional force. Jiu-Jitsu is only purely the gentle art when the techniques are applied with proper execution of balance, timing, and leverage. Without understanding these, it is impossible to use minimum force to create maximum results.

Jiu-Jitsu is one of the oldest forms of martial arts and can be considered the Godfather of all martial arts. Although there have been traces of Jiu-Jitsu being practiced as long as 5,000 years ago, Jiu-Jitsu began to establish itself in Japan in 230 B.C. Jiu-Jitsu became the fighting art of the Samurai in 784 A.D. In the period between the eighth and sixteenth centuries there were many civil wars in Japan, and many systems of Jiu-Jitsu were utilized, practiced, and tested on the battlefield to defeat both armored and armed opponents. Jiu-Jitsu utilized techniques for every situation. These techniques included striking, throwing, grappling, submissions, weapons fighting, and defense. Around 1603 Japan began to enter a fairly peaceful time.

During this time the Japanese continued the practice of Jiu-Jitsu, but because of the increasing immigration of westerners, the Jiu-Jitsu masters were concerned about the bigger and stronger westerners learning the art. Knowing it would be impossible to keep Jiu-Jitsu a secret, they broke it down into several different styles. These styles included techniques that they felt had only limited effectiveness in real combat. Arts like karate, judo, and aikido all derived from Jiu-Jitsu and eventually were transformed into sports in order to keep the most realistic and effective techniques a secret. Although much of Jiu-Jitsu was kept a secret, it was still being practiced behind curtains.

In 1914, a Japanese Jiu-Jitsu and judo instructor by the name of Esai Maeda stopped in Brazil during his World Judo tour. Maeda, also known as "Count Koma," decided to prolong his stay in Brazil to start a Japanese colony in the state of Para in Northern Brazil.

He befriended Gastao Gracie, an influential businessman, who helped the Japanese get established. To show his gratitude, Maeda offered to teach the traditional Japanese Jiu-Jitsu to Gastao's oldest son, Carlos. Carlos eventually began teaching Jiu-Jitsu to his family and established the first Gracie Academy in 1925. Carlos's youngest brother Helio was a physically frail child. He constantly would faint when performing any kind of physical activity. Being forced to only watch Carlos teach Jiu-Jitsu, Helio began to memorize the moves by heart. One day when he was 16 years old, a student showed up for class and Carlos was not around.

Helio, confident to teach, offered to start the class. When the class was over, Carlos showed up apologetic for his delay. The student answered, "No problem. I enjoyed the class with Helio very much and, if you don't mind, I'd like to continue with him." Carlos agreed and Helio became an instructor. He soon realized that some of the techniques he had memorized from watching Carlos teach required too much strength for him to execute. He then started to adapt those moves to his 140-pound frail body and began to improve the leverage in the execution of the techniques. Through trial and error Helio began to break away from the traditional techniques of Jiu-Jitsu and established his own style known as Gracie Jiu-Jitsu.

Continuing to mold Gracie Jiu-Jitsu into a complete self-defense art the Gracie Challenge was formed. This challenge allowed other martial artists to pit themselves against Gracie Jiu-Jitsu to see which style was most effective as well as receive a $10,000 prize if they actually won. Defeating all who came, and many came, the Gracie family remained undefeated in Brazil during the 65 years the Gracie Challenge was active.

In Brazil, Jiu-Jitsu was like football or baseball in the United States. Everyone was acquainted with Jiu-Jitsu and probably trained at some point in their lives. Looking to expand the art of Gracie Jiu-Jitsu, Helio's son Rorion moved to the United States. In 1992 Rorion created an event known as the Ultimate Fighting Championship (UFC). The goal of this event was to have a single-elimination tournament pitting the different styles of martial arts against one another to see which one was the most effective. Rorion was so confident that Gracie Jiu-Jitsu would prevail that the rules of the tournament were simple—no eye-gouging and no biting. This gave all fighters the chance to demonstrate the effectiveness of their art. In fact, there were neither time limits nor weight classes.

Royce Gracie was Rorion's younger brother, and he was the Gracie family member chosen to compete. Royce weighed about 175 pounds and was tall and skinny. Without much more than a scratch on his head, as well as on his opponents head's, Royce submitted all three of his opponents that night in less than five minutes total to become the first Ultimate Fighting Champion. As Royce continued to dominate in the early UFC events, the martial arts world began to crave Gracie Jiu-Jitsu. Now the UFC is no longer style versus style but has become the laboratory for what is known as Mixed Martial Arts. Mixed Martial Arts is a blend of all the effective moves from different martial arts, particularly, Brazilian (Gracie) Jiu-Jitsu, muay thai, kickboxing, and wrestling.

The UFC is one of the most popular sporting events in the world today, and if a fighter isn't well versed in Jiu-Jitsu, his career will be short lived.

One of the beautiful benefits of training in Jiu-Jitsu is that its principles can easily be translated into your everyday living. As stated earlier, Jiu-Jitsu does have an objective, but more important it also has a path. This path, when observed correctly, is what teaches a person not only how to practice Jiu-Jitsu on the mat, but also how to apply it in everyday life.

As the owner of a Mixed Martial Arts Academy in Frederick, Maryland, where I teach Brazilian Jiu-Jitsu, I must not only teach my students the techniques of the art but also lead them down the right path.

Scott Ford has been a Jiu-Jitsu student of mine now for several years. Because Scott and I share both in our faith and our passion for Jiu-Jitsu we have developed a good relationship. With Scott owning his own wealth management firm, he saw how the principles of Jiu-Jitsu made sense in the financial world.

The path is really quite the same. After a few small chats about the idea Scott asked me to help him express the path of Jiu-Jitsu to the world as he would relate it to his financial expertise. Since then we have had multiple discussions about the connection between

Jiu-Jitsu and finances. It has been exciting to be a part of this book and to learn how I can better apply Jiu-Jitsu to my own finances.

I feel sure that you can see the simplicity and effectiveness of the art of Financial Jiu-Jitsu.

LUKE RINEHART
Head Instructor
Clinch Academy

APPENDIX

Seasons of Investing

Many investors focus on determining which stocks or investments to buy, and rightly so: The goal of any investor is to determine which investments will perform well. In simple terms, deciding "what to buy" is a critical task.

So is determining when to sell—in short, following a sell discipline.

For wealth advisors, employing sell discipline is based on constantly monitoring each investment and each client portfolio for any changes that could affect current prospects and future earnings. Sometimes investments have reached a point of maximum, or near-maximum, growth. Other times changes in the economy as a whole dramatically impact the outlook for certain investments. A wealth advisor's goal is to not only select the right securities and investments to buy but also to select the right time to sell. In a larger sense, the goal is to accept small losses in order to avoid large losses.

The goal is not only to grow a client's wealth but also to preserve that wealth.

To accomplish that goal, wealth advisors use a "seasons of investing" approach. Economies are cyclical. Markets are cyclical. One size—one approach—does not fit all. Buy and hold investment strategies work—sometimes. Short-term, opportunistic trading works—sometimes. Good wealth advisors and good investors recognize that markets have seasons, and act accordingly.

To understand the concept of seasons of investing and how investment approaches must adapt to those seasons, let's first take a step back and refute a little conventional wisdom.

Modern Portfolio Theory

Modern Portfolio Theory (MPT), as it has come to be known, was developed by Harry Markowitz. He first published his finance and investing theories in 1952 in the *Journal of Finance*. To say that MPT influenced the world of investing is an understatement; in fact, Markowitz won a Nobel Prize in 1990 for his work.

The data and analysis behind MPT is fairly complicated, but MPT is based on a fairly simple premise. People who believe in Modern Portfolio Theory feel that diversification is the best way to minimize risk, a basic principle I agree with.

Think of it this way: If you invest in only one stock, your risk is that stock will not perform as well as you expect. If the price of the stock falls, you lose money. So what do you do? By investing in more than one stock and diversifying your portfolio, you spread your risk across a number of different investments.

That way you don't have all your eggs in one basket.

One of the goals of MPT is to quantify the benefits of diversification. One of the ways MPT quantifies those benefits is to calculate a deviation from an "average" return. Each stock has its own standard deviation from the "average" return . . . and that deviation is considered to be risk. By creating a blend of stocks in a portfolio, risk can be mitigated.

MPT also assumes that investors act rationally and objectively and that markets are efficient. "Efficient markets" are markets where stocks always trade at a fair value because the price incorporates all existing knowledge and relevant knowledge about that stock. In efficient markets there are no surprises, no inside information . . . stocks are priced "fairly" because investors have access to all the information they need to make smart decisions. That means, of course, that it should be impossible for any investor to outperform the market as a whole, because making smart decisions or timing investments wisely won't matter: The market is efficient.

I think we now know that markets are anything but efficient. Financial returns on individual stocks or even asset classes are not predictable. Individual stock values are not predictable. External economic events can dramatically impact investments. Markets are not always rational. People do not always make rational decisions.

If you like, think of markets as an efficient *process.* Over time markets do tend to sort out the value of stocks. During the Internet bubble, lots of dot-com stocks sold for amazingly high prices, even though the underlying companies were hemorrhaging cash. If you looked at the value of a company like, for example, pets.com, you would say the market was anything *but* efficient. Hype (and hope) led to high stock prices, but when reality set in, some stock prices fell to a realistic value—basically zero. So the process was efficient, because over time the markets did figure out the value of the stocks . . . but in the short term, many investors lost thousands or millions of dollars. Markets are not always rational, and markets are not always efficient—especially in the short term.

Again, I agree with the goal of risk mitigation. The goal is to not only grow a client's wealth but also to preserve his or her capital during down markets and economic downturns. But Modern Portfolio Theory also contains other principles—besides the idea that markets are efficient—that are not useful in today's investing climate.

Historical Data Is . . . Simply History

Economists and financial analysts are consumed by history. They should be; by examining the past we can find clues to the future. But the problem with analyzing historical data, especially over a long time period, is that it can be incredibly misleading.

For example, let's look at the Dow Jones Industrial Average, an average of 30 blue-chip companies considered to be leaders in their industries. The Dow is used as an overall indication of how the stock market is performing.

MPT assumes that a swing of more than 7 percent in the Dow should occur only once every 300,000 years: If the Dow starts the day at 10,000, it should only swing by 700 points once every 300,000 years. Although that sounds predictable and stable, in reality during the last century the Dow experienced 48 days of swings of more than 7 percent.

If you prefer to use odds, Modern Portfolio Theory assumes the odds of a 7 percent drop in one day are 1 in 20 million (those are odds even lottery players might walk away from).

Yet it's happened.

MPT assumes the odds of the Dow falling 7.7 percent in one day are 1 in 50 billion.

That's happened, too.

MPT assumes the odds of the Dow falling 29 percent in one day are 1 in 10 to the 50th power (that's a 1 followed by 50 zeroes).

Yet even that has happened.

Why? Odds and statistics are great, but often statistical analysis is based on historical data and underlying assumptions that don't reflect short-term trends or results, and certainly don't reflect changes in markets, in investing styles, in investment options. . . . When you look back over dozens of years, it's easy to miss the details that make all the difference.

As investors, we're worried about the details—*today*. What happened yesterday (or 50 years ago) is interesting, but what is happening today and what may happen tomorrow are critical.

Buy and Hold

Another underlying principle of Modern Portfolio Theory is that selecting the components of an investment portfolio should be done in two steps:

1. Select investments based on past performance.
2. Refine those choices based on beliefs about future performance.

So far so good, but many investors focus on the first step and ignore the second step. The result is the "buy and hold" investor.

Buy and hold is a long-term investment strategy that assumes that over the long term stocks, investments, and financial markets will provide a decent rate of return. Sure, there will be down markets, and there will be volatile markets . . . but over time the lows will be balanced by the highs. That's why buy-and-hold investors don't focus on investment timing—after all, if you wait long enough, good things happen, right?

In the past that may have been true. If you look at the stock market as a whole over the last 100 years or so, returns average about 10 percent (a number frequently quoted by buy-and-hold investors). The problem is that none of us is likely to be an investor for 100 years; we can't afford to wait until "good things happen." Modern Portfolio Theory recognizes that the past is no indication of the future. That's why the second step is to make choices based on beliefs about future performance.

Buy-and-hold investors, in large part, ignore the second step and focus on the first step. Many financial advisors do the same thing. Regardless of the market, regardless of larger economic trends, many financial advisors use MPT to allocate investments— whether the market is a bull or a bear. Although that sometimes works, especially when the markets are rising (since a rising tide raises all ships), it's a recipe for disaster when markets fall.

Here's a quick example. Keep in mind that the examples that follow are strictly hypothetical and in no way indicate a specific rate of return or specific investments.

In 2008 the Dow reached a high of more than 14,000. For the purpose of this example, I'll assume that your stocks will mirror what happens to the Dow—I'll assume a rational and efficient market. When the Dow was at its high point, your stocks were worth $100,000. Great!

Then the market falls—dramatically. But you're a buy-and-hold investor, so you do nothing. (Short-term blips are no problem, right?) A year later the Dow reaches a low of slightly more than 6,600. The value of your stocks has fallen by more than 50 percent; because the stocks you own mirror those of the Dow, your investments are now worth less than $50,000.

But you hang in there. The economy starts to recover, stock prices start to rise, and a year later the Dow is hovering around the 11,000 mark. Your stocks are now worth more than $78,000—that's much better than your low of $50,000.

But you're also down significantly from your high of $100,000, and several years have passed. Not only have you lost more than $12,000, you've also lost several years worth of potential gains. In real terms you've lost more than $12,000—you've also incurred an opportunity cost. Even if your investments only earned 5 percent, in 2010 your portfolio would be worth more than $110,000. In effect you've lost more than $20,000.

Buy and hold isn't working so well after all.

Now let's take a different approach. I'll stick with my basic assumption that your stocks are worth $100,000 when the Dow reached its high. But instead of ignoring beliefs about future performance, you and your wealth advisor were watching the markets and the economy as a whole and were alert to warning signs. The real estate bubble started to burst in the mid-2000s. Homeowners began defaulting on mortgages. The credit markets began struggling. Yet stocks were significantly overvalued even in the face of serious economic warning signs (proving that the theory of efficient markets is fundamentally flawed).

When the Dow starts to dip, you and your wealth advisor decide to be cautious. You don't sell your stocks right away; you've seen short-term dips before. (Plus, no one has the ability to predict the top or the bottom of any market; the only way to truly determine the top or the bottom is in hindsight.) Over the next few months you both decide that the boom has reached its peak and the short- and long-term economic outlook is negative. In order to preserve capital, you sell your stocks and shift into relatively stable investments when the Dow is at the 12,000 market. Your portfolio was down approximately 14 percent, so you've lost about $14,000. Although that's not a great result, you have managed to preserve the majority of your capital, or $86,000.

But you don't sit idle. You and your wealth advisor watch the markets and the economy. The Dow hits 6,600, but you don't jump back in at that point. You wait until the signs seem right, and you buy the same stocks when the Dow is at 8,000. In the meantime you've made a small return on your investment, so your $86,000 is now worth $90,000. The market continues to rise, and in 2010 your portfolio has risen almost 30 percent, and you now have almost $115,000.

Buy and hold: $78,000.

Capital Preservation Investing: $115,000.

Which portfolio would you choose?

Statistical averages are fun to know, but aren't particularly helpful when you need to make specific investment decisions. The key to smart investing is to make decisions based on market trends. If you simply buy and hold, you enjoy market gains, but you suffer market losses, too. Remember no strategy can guarantee success or prevent loss. The key is to identify trends and adjust investments based on those trends—not to simply buy, hold, and hope.

Seasons of Investing: Challenges and Opportunities

Modern Portfolio Theory and buy-and-hold strategies make sense during bull markets. A rising tide floats all ships. Bull markets come and go, but your need to reach your financial goals is ever-present.

That's why the average investor faces four basic challenges—and those challenges create opportunities.

Challenge 1: Capital Preservation

Buy and hold doesn't work during a bear market. When markets fall, preserving capital should be an investor's main priority. When you lose capital, you not only lose money—you also lose some of your ability to take advantage of future opportunities.

And you also incur an opportunity cost, as mentioned earlier. Say your portfolio is down 40 percent one year and is up 40 percent the next year; you broke even, right? Actually, you didn't. Say your portfolio is worth $100,000. If you lose 40 percent, you're down to $60,000. A 40 percent return on $60,000 is $24,000; although you have made a nice gain, your total portfolio is still only worth

$84,000. In order to "break even," you'll need a return of more than 60 percent. And even if that does happen, while the value of your portfolio has returned to its earlier level, in the meantime you did not earn a return on your investments, plus inflation eroded the value of your portfolio.

In order to offset losses, your portfolio needs to do more than simply break even, especially over the long term.

Capital preservation is a challenge; meet that challenge and you can take advantage of opportunities. As investment analyst Louise Yamada says in her book *Market Magic*, "There are two kinds of losses. A loss of capital and a loss of opportunity; but there will always be another opportunity if you protect capital." You must protect your capital; that way you have capital to invest when new opportunities arise.

There will always be opportunities; to take advantage of those opportunities, you need resources. Capital preservation investing helps ensure that resources are available so you can take advantage of changes in the markets and changes in season.

Challenge 2: Seasons of Investing

Markets have seasons. Think of seasons as broken into two parts: Spring and summer, when values rise, and fall and winter when values fall. Over the past 100 years, the stock market has experienced seven major seasons, the seventh being the season we are currently "enjoying." Seasons tend to last between 8 and 25 years, with the spring and summer seasons tending to be shorter in duration. (In other words, bear markets tend to last longer than bull markets.)

What causes seasons? There are a variety of reasons, but a simple way to view market seasonality is to look at price-to-earnings ratios. Price-to-earnings ratio (P/E) is a basic financial measurement that compares a company's stock price to its earnings per share. For example, if a stock is currently trading at $10 per share and its earnings per share are $1, then the P/E ratio for that stock is 10, or $10 divided by $1. In general terms, a higher P/E ratio indicates that investors think earnings will grow in the future, making the company and its stock more valuable. A low P/E ratio indicates investors think earnings will stay flat or possibly even fall. But remember that P/E ratios vary by industry; P/E ratios in some industries, like high-tech, tend to be fairly high, while P/E ratios in major industrial companies tend to be low.

Even so, P/E ratios tend to be one of the leading measurements of stock values because they can help predict future stock prices.

In simple terms, when P/E ratios rise, stock prices also rise; when that happens, we are in a spring and summer season, and the rising tide will float almost all ships higher.

When P/E ratios fall, we enter a fall and winter season, and stock prices fall because the falling tide lowers all ships.

When you recognize the change in season . . .

Challenge 3: Identify Seasonal Transitions

Preserving capital by following a sell discipline—and also making smart buy decisions—is based on predicting where the markets are likely to go. A key to making smart predictions is to identify transitions between seasons. I use a variety of research and analytical tools to identify both the investment seasons and the signs of a transition between those seasons. Quite frankly, correctly identifying seasonal transitions is probably beyond the skills or capabilities of the average investor; staying on top of the markets is a full-time job for skilled financial analysts. But identifying the transitions creates opportunities to preserve capital and then take advantage of market upswings; timing is critical.

Why? To do well, you need to beat the averages.

Challenge 4: Beat the "Average"

Each of us has a different investing time frame. If you are 20 years old, you have 40 to 60 years of investing ahead of you. If you are in your fifties, your time frame is naturally shorter. That's another reason why MPT and buy-and-hold strategies are theories that don't work in practice for real investors.

Modern Portfolio Theory is based on a 75- to 100-year time frame; over that period of time it "works." But do you have 100 years to wait for MPT to work for you?

As I mentioned earlier, the stock market has historically averaged a 10 percent return. Some years were better and worse than others, though. More than half the time the market has fallen or risen more than 16 percent in any one period. If the market beats the average, great—but if it drops during your investing time frame, the effect can be devastating, especially if you can't wait 10 or 20 years for things to "average out." Seasons tend to last for a number of years; can you afford to wait 15 to 20 years for fall and winter to turn to spring and summer?

Invest with the Seasons

So what can you do? Adapting investing decisions based on seasons can help preserve capital as well as optimize returns. Again, in general terms:

During *spring and summer* a modified buy-and-hold approach makes sense. When the broader market rises, the goal as a wealth advisor is to take advantage of a bull market and not only enjoy the upswing but also work hard to beat the markets.

During *fall and winter* a dynamic management approach makes sense. The goal is to preserve capital and then make investments that take advantage of what opportunities do exist even during a bear market.

How does that work? First, I follow the basic steps in the Way2Wealth. I help my clients determine what True Wealth means to them and make sure that they thoroughly understand their goals. I then help clients analyze their current positions and establish their family benchmarks.

Then I apply a capital preservation approach to building wealth:

- Base investment portfolios on economic analysis and long-term uptrends.
- Monitor legal insider trading activity to verify trends.
- Identify the best investment vehicles to take advantage of economic conditions and long-term uptrends.
- Buy and sell by using quantitative analysis tools, ensuring that emotion is not a driver of investment decisions.

Sound simple? It is—and it isn't. To make the approach more clear, let's take a look at the recent market downturn and steps a theoretical investor might have taken.

When a market falls, preserving capital is critical. Two ways to preserve capital and continue to grow wealth is to convert stock investments into cash or alternative asset classes. (That's why we like to think of our approach as a "Capital Preservation Model with an Offensive Strategy.")

Converting to cash is a simple premise to understand. If the market falls and you shift investments to cash-based securities like treasury bills or money market funds, you both preserve capital and are also poised to better take advantage of future market upswings.

Alternative asset classes include:

- Private equity
- Hedge funds
- Venture capital
- Absolute return strategies
- Real estate
- Commodities
- And so on

Alternative asset investments can be a part of any diversified investment portfolio, in any season. Alternative investments might not be suitable for all investors, as the strategies employed in the management of some alternative investments may accelerate the velocity of potential loss. But alternative investments can be especially important during fall and winter, when stock investments are generally unlikely to yield a reasonable return and may in fact be incredibly risky.

So what could our theoretical investor have done?

After identifying a seasonal transition, the first step might have been to convert a large portion of his stock investments into cash; that way capital is preserved and a variety of investing options remain open.

For the remaining stock investments, that portfolio is actively managed, possibly including:

- More frequent portfolio rebalancing.
- A focus on dividend-yielding stocks.
- Writing options to generate additional return.
- Overall active management of individual stocks and the portfolio as a whole.

Then a portion of the cash might be invested in alternative strategies. A portion may be invested in commodities. A portion may be used to invest in a start-up or small business. The investor may decide to purchase real estate, especially if he feels the real estate market is poised for an upswing.

In short, during fall and winter the investor seeks to preserve capital while taking advantage of other opportunities to build wealth.

The goal is to grow your portfolio and your wealth—regardless of the season.

The Seasonal Approach

Seasonal investing is based on a relatively simple premise: When the sun is shining almost anyone can make hay. When winter comes . . . it's not so easy.

During a bull market, the average investor enjoys a reasonable return. Smart investors enjoy better than reasonable returns, and while diversification does not guarantee against loss, in most cases an investor who creates a relatively diversified portfolio can enjoy a decent return on his or her investment.

But when summer turns to fall and then winter, the average investor—and the average investor's wealth advisor—tends to take a beating. Emotion tends to play a fairly large role, because most people hope to overcome their losses. Many investors are often hesitant to sell a stock that has fallen in price; they want to "make back their losses." I understand the feeling but disagree completely with the strategy.

For example, say you purchase 1,000 shares of stock at $30 per share. Your total investment is $30,000. If the stock falls to $25 per share, you've lost $5,000. If you're like many investors, the thought of taking a loss is incredibly painful, so you hang on to the stock.

And you wait.

And wait.

If after a year the stock does happen to increase in price, you may make up some or all of your losses, but keep in mind that the stock will have to rise to a price over $30 per share for you to break even because your loss includes an opportunity cost as well as the effect of inflation. And what if the stock does not rise in value, or even continues to fall? At some point you may eventually decide to sell . . . but at what eventual cost to you?

Investors who take a seasonal approach evaluate the market's season as well as the future prospects for individual stocks. If the stock price has fallen because of a fundamental weakness in the economy or in the company's prospects or business model, selling the stock—even at a loss—may be the best way to preserve the remaining capital and free up those funds to make other more profitable investments. As an investor, your goal is to achieve a return equal to or higher than your Family Benchmark on your total investments, not just on each individual stock or investment vehicle. When a stock price falls, emotion can take over. Most people don't like to lose, and when you sell at a lower price than what you paid, losing converts from being a paper loss to an official loss. Many people focus on paper losses or paper gains, but at the end of the day your investment portfolio still has an actual and absolute value—your goal is to grow that actual value and reach your investing goals.

Investing based on seasons requires an ability to not only understand the current season but to forecast transitions in seasons so that you can be poised to take full advantage of that transition. But the seasonal approach does require a lot of hard work. Buy-and-hold strategies are relatively easy to follow. (Any strategy based on hope instead of research and analysis is an easy strategy to follow.)

Modern Portfolio Theory and buy-and-hold strategies only work in theory, and the latter is incredibly long term; your portfolio—and your future—is anything but theoretical and matters to you and your time frame.

Wealth advisors' goals are to work hard to actively manage portfolios so clients can preserve capital while also growing their portfolios, regardless of the season. Theories are fine, strategies are interesting . . . but flexibility, adaptability, objectivity, and hard work make all the difference.

Theories are interesting.

Results are all that matter.

About the Author

Scott Ford

Besides being a Brazilian Jiu-Jitsu aficionado, Scott Ford is president and founder of Cornerstone Wealth Management Group in Hagerstown, Maryland. He is frequently featured in the media and in speaking engagements, promoting his trademark philosophy known as the "Six Pillars of Life"—a strategy designed to balance one's spirituality, family, health, career, philanthropy, and finances.

Scott utilized this same philosophy as a foundation in developing Way2Wealth—his unique and comprehensive financial planning process found in this book. When applied, this process results in the creation of individualized financial strategies designed to increase the probability that people can achieve their financial objectives. Scott believes that this aids in eliminating the distractions people face in today's chaotic financial environment.

With a focus on community involvement and activism, the proceeds from his first book, *The Widow's Wealth Map: Six Steps to Beginning Again,* were donated to a variety of local charities. He has also been a guest on NBC and has been featured in the *New York Times, Christian Science Monitor, InvestmentNews* and has contributed to the *Today Show.*

Scott is a registered representative with LPL Financial, the nation's largest independent Broker/Dealer and is ranked in the top 1 percent of all advisors (based on gross dealer commissions).

Index